A BETTER TEN COMMANDMENTS

A GUIDE TO LIVING LIFE WITH, AND ON PURPOSE

JAMES MILLER

www.ABetterTen.com

For my Nephews
Josh and Cash

CONTENTS

THE COMMANDMENTS vii
THE BIRTH OF A BOOK ix
CLEARING THE PATH xiii

BE THE BEST VERSION OF THYSELF 1
DISCOVER SERENITY 9
LOVE SELFLESSLY 16
PRACTICE POSITIVE RECIPROCITY 22
FIND PERSPECTIVE 28
BE GRATEFUL 35
CULTIVATE A RATIONAL COMPASSION 40
CHOOSE GROWTH 47
BALANCE 52
KNOW IT'S ALWAYS NOW 56
EPILOGUE 64

SO ... WHAT NOW? ... WHAT COMES NEXT? 69
BIBLIOGRAPHY 71
REFERENCES 73

THE COMMANDMENTS

THOU SHALT:

I
BE THE BEST VERSION OF THYSELF

II
DISCOVER SERENITY

III
LOVE SELFLESSLY

IV
PRACTICE POSITIVE RECIPROCITY

V
FIND PERSPECTIVE

VI
BE GRATEFUL

VII
CULTIVATE A RATIONAL COMPASSION

VIII
CHOOSE GROWTH

IX
FIND BALANCE

X
KNOW IT'S ALWAYS NOW

THE BIRTH OF A BOOK

I vividly remember sitting in my parents' driveway, fondling my father's pistol and contemplating the best way to end my pain. I was nineteen years old, and I absolutely hated myself. I felt like a social outcast and had no idea who I wanted to be, what I wanted to do, and certainly no idea what truly mattered.

At a pivotal time when you're supposed to venture out into the world and form the vital bonds beyond those of your immediate family, I was shrinking further and further into avoidance and despair. I was supposed to be learning life's most important lessons, but my all-consuming negative thoughts were pushing me deeper into the abyss. I only wanted to hide, I only wanted to ease my pain.

Growing up, I struggled to connect with my family, and the hatred for my father at the time was a shining example. The rest of my relationships were at best functional, and at worst destructive. I couldn't find a community of people I could relate to, and I had an inherent distaste for social cliques and all things religious. Most importantly, I struggled with who I was as a person and whom I wanted to become.

My parents weren't oblivious to my difficulties, but they didn't realize the depth of my despair. They asked if I wanted help; they asked if I wanted to talk to a professional, but being the stubborn person I was, I mistakenly believed that I alone could find the solutions to my problems. I decided that the best course of action was to shut out my emotions and operate on a purely logical basis. And, for almost twenty years, it seemed to have worked.

I did my best to find and follow what I thought to be the wisest path. I built what seemed from the outside to be an envious life. I earned six figures and only worked 150 hours a year. I was on track to replace my income and retire as a millionaire at the ripe old age of forty-five. I was traveling the world and doing many of the things I had always wanted to do, and there were elements of my life that truly made me proud. I'd discovered some solutions to big problems that many people tend to struggle with. I'd built a healthy relationship with money and knew what to use it for. I valued my time and was pretty good at spending it wisely.

But something was still missing. I was still struggling to bring the answers I did know into alignment with a grand, unified theory. I was still failing to find deep and meaningful connections with many of the people and things that truly matter in life. In other words, I didn't feel the joy of being – just momentary glimpses of what was possible.

As early as I can remember, I always wanted good reasons for what I thought. I always wanted to be able to validate my statements and actions with proof. I always knew that nothing should be taken on faith alone. Unfortunately this way of thinking tended to ostracize me from many people in my life and every religion I had encountered up to that point. Of course, I didn't have all the answers at that time, nor do I have all of them now, but somewhere deep inside, I knew what I truly wanted. Deep down, I knew that the answers to most of life's fundamental questions were out there. Some part of me knew that I could lead a life of purpose and meaning without taking anything on faith.

I read and explored, experimented and failed. I pursued my intrigue and curiosity. I dug deeply into any endeavor that showed promise and courageously leapt into the chasm of my own ignorance. I willingly incorporated new ideas and was unafraid to change my mind. I devoured everything I could get my hands on, and I knew that I could never give up. *A Better Ten Commandments* was born as a result.

Given the controversial nature of religion and ethics, this book will undoubtedly offend many people. My intent, however, is not to offend any person of faith. I do not wish to denigrate any of the beautiful and timeless wisdom found within a faith. My goal is to criticize faith itself. My goal is to apply the pressures of reason, skepticism, and critical thinking. My goal is to apply the processes that truly free humanity from our own ignorance and to help people find fulfillment without bondage to religious dogmas.

I want to keep all of humanity's timeless lessons, including those from faith. I want to keep every valuable piece of wisdom from every field of human inquiry. I want everyone to lead a life of purpose and meaning. If you want to believe something and your beliefs have no consequence on the remainder of society, I implore you to keep them.

However, pressure must be applied to the ideas that are not conducive to creating lives that are truly worth living. Pressure must be applied to the ideas that are not helping us create a durable, just, and global society. Pressure must be applied in order for us to reach our true potential. Amongst being many other things, this book is a form of pressure.

A Better Ten Commandments is also guide. A guide that will help illuminate the path to building a meaningful life. This book is a brief and hopefully poignant explanation of all the wisdom I discovered on my quest to living a life with, and on, purpose. This book is my answer to what truly matters. Writing this story and learning these lessons helped save my life.

What is more, I know that this book can help someone in need. I know that the lessons contained within it can make someone's life better. I know that this book can help save someone's life. But only you can decide if that person is you.

My purpose as an author, as in life, is to increase the sum fulfillment of everyone I interact with in every possible way I can. My legacy is to help you enjoy your life to its utmost potential and to have you share that enjoyment with others. My life's work is to make the world a better place in whatever capacity I can.

I hope for only good things on your journey and that you find this book useful. If you do, I only ask that you share it with others you think may find it useful as well. My vision is to have this story help as many people in the world as possible.

As the Buddha said, "Thousands of candles can be lit from a single one, and the life of that candle will not be diminished. Happiness only increases by being shared."

And the only way to make that happen...is to begin.
James Miller
August 11th, 2017

CLEARING THE PATH

The title, *A Better Ten Commandments,* is intentionally provocative. I want to challenge preconceived notions and convince you that there are better rules to live by than "God's top ten." I want to encourage the idea that beliefs have consequences. I want to challenge the notion that it is taboo to criticize belief. I want to leave a legacy. I want to be relevant. I also want to become the exemplar of enlightenment and the 374th most interesting person on the planet (someone has to, I figure it may as well be me). But ultimately, this book isn't about what I want. It's about what we all want.

So who is this story for? Who truly needs this book? In a certain sense, it's for everyone. Ask yourself, what is it that we all truly want? My answer is this book, A guide to living life with and on purpose. Though I realize some will disagree, I'm confident enough to say it anyway, in fact, I invite the challenge. How else do we temper our personal and collective intellect? But to answer the question more specifically, this book is for anyone who wants to lead a more authentic and compelling life. It's for those struggling to find meaning and morality in a confusing and often chaotic world. It's for those who feel disillusioned by the hypocrisy and contradictory nature of their religious texts or community. It's for those who want rational reasons to justify the rules by which they live. And most importantly it is for anyone who wants a deeper understanding of what truly matters in life.

I know that we are perpetually at an inflection point, both in our lives and in history. As stewards of this planet, I believe it is one of our primary duties to make the most of the opportunities and talents bestowed upon us by nature. I believe it is imperative that we do all in our power to change ourselves and the world for the better. Wouldn't you agree that making the most of life is in our best interest?

Of course, in order to get somewhere you must first choose a path. Furthermore, if nothing matters, then there is nothing to save. This book, therefore, is a compendium of ten great ideas, ten ideas that rational thought can justify, ten ideas that have stood the test of time, ten ideas that truly matter and can be used as a guide. These ten ideas are a foundational framework for who you should be on a daily basis; they are commandments that work together and build upon each other in order for you to lead a more abundant, fulfilling, and meaningful life.

In order to clear the way for these timeless lessons, and how to best utilize them, not only will we have to address the severe limitations of the original Ten Commandments, but we'll also have to spend some time discussing the topics of philosophy, ethics, religion, and who we are as human beings into the bulk of this part of the book. I hope you'll understand that covering these, and a few other related topics, will take more than a page or two. Suffice it to say ... I will get to the point.

I imagine a thought may have already crossed your mind; who does this guy think he is, saying he knows better than God? Well, first, the lessons contained in this book actually help you become a better person. Second, I thoroughly enjoy the irony inherent in the faithful preaching the virtues of love, tolerance, and forgiveness, then touting the condemnation of all non-believers to an eternity of hellfire. Last, and certainly not least, I'm not afraid to have an opinion on the matter, as I don't believe in imaginary friends (insert random god) meting out justice in the here and now or deciding my fate after the death of my brain.

So how did we get here? How did we find ourselves in a world listening to men in funny hats and silly dresses blather on about how the great juju in the sky helped them find their car keys and contentment? How did we end up in a world where a man like Joshua Milton Blahyi, popularly known as "General Butt Naked," could enlist children as soldiers, then cannibalize and offer them as a blood sacrifice, and be responsible for the death of at least 20000 people, yet go on to start a ministry preaching the gospel of Christ and expect to be redeemed, not only by his victims, but by the creator of the universe for eternity? How did it come to pass that people could believe that no matter how atrocious your actions, you need only accept Christ and all is forgiven? This type of morality is disgusting and should be considered unconscionable, but I've digressed.

The short answer to how we got here is assuredly evolution, both biological and social. When you understand the "lowly stamp of our origin," it illuminates a significant void in the vast chasm that is our ignorance and ineptitude. Evolution is a beacon of hope for humanity – a beacon that will help guide our understanding of who we are and what is possible; a beacon that will illuminate the path to creating a durable, just, and global civilization. But, this isn't a book about evolution; it's a story. A story of finding and forgiving our many faults, a story of cultivating love and hope, and ultimately, if we do what is necessary, a story of redemption.

Of course, every hero story needs a villain, and for our purposes, that enemy is something that lies at the very core of most religions – an issue that will ultimately bring about religion's inevitable demise. That issue is dogma, proclamations of truth without the benefit of evidence. I readily concede that within the bounds of every faith I've considered there are truths that are well worth knowing and incorporating into your life; truths that are fundamental to leading a beautiful and meaningful existence. Unfortunately, however, these truths are obscured and inexorably entangled in tenets of faith that are at best baseless, and at worst vile and unimaginable.

If you have a problem with me questioning people's faiths, let me attempt to appease your concerns. If you believe that mustard is the greatest condiment in the world or that Willie Nelson is the most talented singer ever, I have no issue with your faith. If your belief only brings joy to your life, I implore you, believe to your heart's content. If, however, your beliefs affect the law, if your beliefs have an impact on other people's lives, I must take issue. How we govern our lives must operate on an empirical basis. We must have good reasons to say the things we say and do the things we do.

Indoctrination

How did we get so hopelessly tangled in the weaving webs of dogma in the first place? Most people, through no fault of their own, are indoctrinated as children or young adults to believe a certain set of ideas prior to developing their ability to think critically or question those ideas. Think of Unicorns, Sasquatch, Santa Claus, and child suicide bombers. Gladly, most parents have the sense to stop lying to their children about most of these things.

What is more, religiosity, just like any other trait, is highly heritable. Combine that with our brain's ability to confabulate and make false positives, and we have a wonderful recipe for making mistakes. Nature evolved a system to be right enough for survival, not a perfect logic machine.

Some believers find meaning and morality in religious texts by cherry-picking passages that add value to their lives while simultaneously ignoring or baselessly rationalizing those that don't. Holding mutually incompatible ideas is known as cognitive dissonance. Such as someone suggesting they believe God is all-powerful and at the same time believing they have free will. Those two ideas cannot exist simultaneously.

Others affirm or adopt their faith through a multitude of other factors or a combination thereof; spiritual experience, culture, fear, death, social exclusion, guilt, communal bonding, dissatisfaction with their current reality, or their unwillingness to admit ignorance. By no means is this an exhaustive list but it certainly represents a fair share of the causes for which people mistakenly fall prey to faith.

This book is a direct challenge to the very idea of faith and the individuals and organizations that use it for ill will. It is also a statement that we know better, or at the very least, we should. It is my assertion that it is OUR duty, not a deity's, to make the most of our lives and this world. Furthermore, if you believe the Ten Commandments are a perfect distillation of ethics and haven't any room for improvement, you really should take it upon yourself to read some other holy books.

Dismissing God's Rules

As for "God's" rules, let me briefly dismiss them as irrelevant or inefficient. But before we do that, let's review what the "Good Book" actually says on the matter, for the Ten Commandments that most people are familiar with are a bit more discordant than people tend to believe. If you re-read Exodus, you'll find that originally the laws were spoken to Moses by God and repeated to the Israelites as narrative. The second time Moses sat down with the boss, he was gone for forty days and nights, and when he came back with the first set of tablets, he found the Israelites partying like it was 1999 BC and paying homage to a golden calf. He went bridezilla and broke the tablets and had the Israelites kill 3000 of their brethren. I understand we all need to let off a little steam now and again, but wow. And by the way, didn't he forget the whole "thou shalt not kill" rule?

Following this bloodbath, Moses went back to the head cheese to get the actual Ten Commandments. Let us read. In Exodus 34, you'll discover that thou shalt: 1. Worship no other Gods 2. Make no molten Gods 3. Keep the feast of unleavened bread 4. Offer the first-born ox or sheep to Yahweh 5. Work six days and rest on the seventh 6. Observe the festival of weeks 7. Visit Yahweh three times a year 8. Not use leaven when offering a blood sacrifice to Yahweh 9. Give the first fruits you bear to Yahweh, and to bring Gods treatise to a close, 10. Not boil a baby goat in its mother's milk. And if they did all that, Yahweh, acting as a divine real estate broker, would drive out the Amorites, Canaanites, Hittites, Perizzites, Hivites, and Jebusites so that the Israelites may occupy already settled land. Interesting. Hopefully you think, as I do, that these rules mostly discount themselves.

As for discounting the modern idea of the Ten Commandments, rules one through four have nothing to do with morality or leading a meaningful life, and are purely a product of culture. If you need a refresher, they are: 1. No other gods 2. Not taking Gods name in vain 3. No graven images, and 4. No working on the Sabbath. Thankfully, we no longer think you should be put to death for praying to Poseidon, saying "God damn it," whittling a sculpture of your imaginary friend, or working on Sunday. You may want to speak with a mental health professional about each of these proclivities, but death seems a bit harsh.

Contrary to "God's" first four Commandments, thousands of societies having existed in ignorance of the Judeo/Christian revelation or prior to it managed to create their own gods and rules. Don't you find it odd that "God" did not or could not tell everyone on the planet his rules? Rather, he decided to only share his message with a small group of displaced migrants lost in the desert. There is consensus amongst historians and archeologists that there's absolutely no evidence the "exodus" and wandering described in the bible even took place. So, doesn't it make more sense that the Israelites, just like every other culture in history, borrowed and adapted or fabricated their own rules and creation myth?

Commandments five through nine can be stated in a single sentence and are common sense. If you need a refresher, they are: 5. Thou shalt honor thy father and thy mother 6. Thou shalt not kill 7. Thou shalt not commit adultery 8. Thou shalt not steal, and 9. Thou shalt not bear false witness. All but a few civilizations throughout history have managed to figure out that being nice to your parents is good and that murder, adultery, theft, and lying are bad. (Commandment nine is technically perjury, but I've taken the liberty of elucidating on the deeper principle of lying.) Not only are these and other ethical mores patently and intuitively obvious, but their existence also predates biblical times in Sumerian, Babylonian, Egyptian, and other eastern codes of conduct. What is more, and as I will explain later, to some extent, they even predate humanity itself. (I do hope to keep you engaged, but, when you have a moment look up Frans de Waal's fairness study, it makes my point obvious)

Beyond the previously mentioned issues, most rules typically have reasonable exceptions. Examples, you ask? Put yourself in the shoes of Elisabeth Fritzl, held captive for twenty-four years, physically and sexually abused, and mothering seven children, all her father's doing. Shall she honor him? Who wouldn't kill a Mao, Stalin, Pol Pot, or Hitler without a fair trial? What if you've been forced into an emotionally and physically abusive marriage and manage to escape without divorce? How about refusing to steal the Enigma Machine that coded orders for the Nazi's? Lastly, Jeffrey Dahmer's final victim lied to him in order to escape, getting Dahmer caught in the process; would you rather have him end up in Dahmer's freezer or worse yet, continue to have Dahmer at large?

And how about the tenth Commandment, "Thou shalt not covet?" Thought crimes? Seriously? What if I covet one of my neighbor's cookies and I ask nicely or offer to pay? Or better yet, what if my neighbors give away ninety percent of their earnings to charity and I want to emulate their lifestyle? For one, it's impossible to even prevent thoughts from arising into consciousness in the first place. And second, ask yourself, should it really be a crime to simply want something?

Remember, these are supposedly the only rules physically written by God himself. One would think they'd be the most immutable, prophetic, profound, and meaningful words ever written in any language, but they seem rather pedestrian. If someone such as myself can point out the rather obvious fallibility of these rules, how can we be expected to believe that the creator of the universe forged them?

The limitations of the Ten Commandments being rather obvious, it must be said that religious customs, culture, and many of our ethical mores are born out of thousands of years of shared experience, and they needn't be discarded on a whim. Many are prescient, poetic, wise, and still true, and they need to be encouraged and retained. Oftentimes, they stymie progress for a good reason, as we have tendencies towards overconfidence in the solutions born out of our perceived intellectual prowess. But there are cultural and customary residues that need to be washed away, and this book is a form of soap.

The Difficulty of Being Right

We all know that life can be difficult, and one of the main

causes is that reliably separating fact from fiction is a difficult endeavor. Within any particular line of reasoning, it only takes one mistake to arrive at the wrong conclusion. Furthermore, as additional conditions are applied, the complexity of the problem grows exponentially. Now compound these with other easily demonstrable issues; our intuition, for instance, is often a poor guide to how things actually are. What is more, wrong answers outnumber right ones by an incomprehensible margin, and worse yet some of those wrong answers can have very compelling reasons. It's no wonder we struggle with the riddles of our existence.

Have you ever seen a person searching for their glasses, only to find them on their forehead, or dangling around their neck? How about when you're looking for something in the fridge, only to find it staring you directly in the face? If we can be fooled so easily, how can we then assume that anyone knows the mind of God, or that Jesus was the son of God, or that Mohammad flew to heaven on a winged horse, or what happens to your consciousness after death? It's simply preposterous for anyone to make such outlandish claims.

Another enormous issue with how we deem our morality and ethical standards is that of philosophy. We typically find ourselves divided between two opposing views. Though you may be unfamiliar with their creators or methodology, the deontology of Immanuel Kant and the utilitarianism of Jeremy Bentham are widely held views. But you'll typically find yourself struggling to find the happy medium between them, as neither is ideal.

Deontology is the world of absolutes, and a deontologist would argue that certain actions are always right or wrong no matter the outcome. The Ten Commandments are examples of this line of thinking. Utilitarianism, on the other hand, is the world of consequences, and proponents of this philosophy argue for the greatest good for the greatest number. The previously mentioned exceptions to the Ten Commandments would be a wonderful set of examples.

There are numerous creative thought experiments that elucidate the dubious nature of each philosophy, the most common of which is the trolley scenario. In the experiment, you are a trolley operator, and a specific trolley carrying five passengers has lost its brakes. If the trolley continues on its current track, it will kill all aboard. With the push of a button you can alter the trolleys course saving the five, but by taking this action, one innocent bystander will be killed. Do you push the button?

Subtle changes to the thought experiment replace the switch by having you push the bystander into the path of the trolley to alter its course; others replace the bystander with someone you know or something of great value that belongs to you. The findings from these experiments are intriguing and of course limited, as there is a gap between what people do in the lab and what they do in real life. If you're curious, however, most people push the button but wouldn't push the bystander. Scary, but anonymity matters (to ourselves at least).

In film and print, this moral dilemma is often on display. For instance, take the wonderful example from *The Imitation Game*. A team of prodigies lead by Alan Turing succeeded in the seemingly impossible task of breaking the code of the enigma machine, which was used for every electronic Nazi command. Once the code was broken, however, they didn't stop every attack. They kept the decoded orders a secret and only utilized the most critical pieces using mathematical probabilities, thereby turning the tide of the war. They deliberately let thousands die in order to save millions.

When this act of sacrifice is consensual, it is considered an act of heroism. When it is not, we question the ethics of the decision maker or person committing the act. This is the conundrum we find ourselves in; we wish the world operated on absolutes, but unfortunately, the ends sometimes do justify the means.

Another issue in the field of ethics and morality is our emotionality. For instance, when considering any proposition, studies have shown that be it a news story, a painting, or a thought experiment in ethics, prior to our level of awareness, our brain makes a judgment call – either like or dislike. After this emotional assessment, people then latch onto arguments or confabulate reasons that support their subconscious feelings in order to justify their position. As an example, when I ask if you think private masturbation or recreational drug use is wrong, whether you realize it or not, you will have a visceral reaction that will affect how you answer that question.

But feelings are not the same as empirical reasons and should hold virtually no weight when considering a proposition's truth. For example, Ghengis Khan was reported to have said that, "A man's greatest pleasure is to defeat his enemies, to drive them before him, to take from them that which they possessed, to see those whom they cherished in tears, to ride their horses, and to hold their wives and daughters in his arms." Just because something feels good, that doesn't make it right.

Of course, emotionality is a primary driving force in how we live our lives, and the world would be a terribly boring place without them. But it is reason, skepticism, and the scientific method that shed light on the truth, and they are sorely needed to help defend against our propensity to err in our judgments and guide our emotionality in a positive direction. As Benjamin Franklin said, "If passion drives, let reason hold the reins."

Our cognitive biases also play havoc on us reaching rationally justifiable positions. An entire book could be written on these mental shortcomings, but here is a brief list of examples. The confirmation bias, where we tend to only reference or pay attention to information that confirms our previously held position and avoid information that disagrees or disproves our thoughts on a given subject. The probability bias, by which we ignore readily available and obvious statistical data that disproves our position. The negativity bias, when we are presented with two equivalent outcomes, one good and one bad, and we tend to place more emphasis on the negative. The bandwagon bias, where the probability of a person accepting a proposition, true or not, increases based on the number of people who already hold that position. The all-familiar placebo effect, when simply believing something will have an effect is enough to create such effect. And my personal favorite, the blind spot bias, where you simply fail to recognize that you have any cognitive biases at all. These and other biases are great hurdles in intellectual honesty, but as time goes on, we will discover and implement ways to protect against our obvious fallibility as rational agents.

Another issue with morality is subjectivity versus objectivity. If our feelings, attitudes, and beliefs are to decide what actions are right and wrong, then morality becomes subjective and therefore just opinion. If the Nazis won WWII and killed all dissenters, that would be subjectively good if you happened to be a Nazi. If what the Nazis did was objectively wrong, then it was wrong regardless of what anyone thinks, feels or believes, and regardless of who won the war. Religious thinkers typically pass the objectivity buck to God, making moral truths objective to us but subjective to God. I think, however, that ethics can operate just like chemistry or biology. Many of our ethical and unethical behaviors are biologically or socially evolved; other ethical standards were created through the power of rationality, public discourse, and social discovery. Ask yourself, where did our laws, courts, jails, police, military, and governments come from? We created them through a vast network of history, ethical impulses, culture, thought, and, most importantly, results.

We decide what is right, we decide what is fair, and we decide what is and what is not acceptable behavior. That may sound subjective, but many of these principles operate on objective truths – truths that encourage a more just and egalitarian society; truths based on our values of maximizing human fulfillment and decreasing human suffering. Is a world where lying, cheating, raping, murder, and stealing are encouraged objectively worse? Is the representative democracy objectively better than a tyrannical autocracy? Is it better to live a longer, healthier, and happier life? I hope the answers to those questions are obvious; if not, we need to have a chat.

Of course, enriching the quality of an individual, let alone all of humanity, is a notoriously difficult task, but we needn't assume that it's beyond our capability or that we haven't made progress on multiple fronts. There are better and worse ways to live, and we must endeavor to discover and encourage those ways.

As we progress, I believe a science of morality will emerge and grow. Objective truths, beyond those we've already discovered or confirmed, about how to best function as a human being within a society will be discovered and hopefully implemented into our laws, homes, and educational systems. Over time we will uncover more ways to increase the aggregate fulfillment and reduce the sum suffering of humanity. We may discover that there are multiple right answers to moral questions and that those answers depend on the situation and the individuals involved. Science is, after all, probabilistic. Just as our understanding of every other endeavor we've undertaken has progressed, we will gradually unravel how best to live a human life. But until that time comes, we must rely on a combination of history, philosophy, culture, law, and, of course, the stories we tell ourselves.

The Origin of Ethics

Where do our morals come from? What is the origin of our ethics? Most religious thinkers tend to believe that they must have been given to us by divine command. There are many problems with this theory of course, i.e. which god's divine command, the disturbing nature of many commands, the interpretation of said commands, the contradictory nature of certain commandments with others, the hypocrisy of a god breaking his/her own commandments, the irony that man has written all of them, and, as Plato pointed out, the possibility that the gods had no choice. But if you studied the matter further by reading a few evolutionary biology and psychology books, you'd understand that most social behaviors, both ethical and disturbing, predate humanity and have either been observed in nature or demonstrated in the lab. Bats practice reciprocity through the sharing of blood. Birds lie by sounding fake warnings of danger in order to steal food. Rats given the opportunity to eat chocolate or help another rat under distress help their fellow rat then go a step further and share the chocolate. Monkeys will forego food in order to prevent the shocking of another monkey. More examples in the animal kingdom include: displeasure with the unequal division of food, deeming social hierarchy, sexual jealousy, competition, punishment, cooperation, altruism, empathy, murder, a sense of equal pay for equal work, and the list goes on and on.

If you prefer only human examples, read the fascinating *Just Babies: The Origins of Good and Evil* by Paul Bloom, in which he discusses the origins of many of the traits we'd describe as moral and immoral based on studies of infants. One-year-olds will dole out rewards to puppets that share and take away rewards from puppets that steal. Some will go even further and try to punish the thief by hitting them. Toddlers, without being prompted or trained, will assist a stranger that has their hands full by opening a door. I imagine I don't have to tell you that they've not found the time or inclination to read the Bible just yet.

On the other hand, and unfortunately, we also come hardwired with a number of negative traits including overt selfishness, disgust, aggression, and in-group out-group mentalities. Of course, not all morality is genetic, proof being in the fact that children can be indoctrinated to believe just about anything. My thinking on the matter is that there is vast continuum between genetic traits and cultural byproducts and that each has its influence to a greater or lesser degree. For instance, your eye color is almost purely genetic but can change subtly through environmental factors that influence gene expression. On the other hand, there's suicide bombing, which is almost purely cultural, though specific genetic dispositions may be influential or necessary, such as high levels of aggression and impressionability. This is, of course, the old nature vs. nurture argument, and both must have an impact. But regardless of a trait's origin, be it nature or nurture, if we are to flourish as a society, one of our highest endeavors should be to discover and encourage all that we understand to ultimately be fulfilling, and at the same time discourage all that we understand increases the sum suffering of the world.

Where Do We Go from Here

Given all of this, what rules should we follow? What rules should we hold sacred, or at the very least strive to hold ourselves accountable to? First, they must be sustainable. If a rule can't perpetually be followed, how could it ever be expected to work in the long run? Second, they must be able to stand the pressures of skepticism, reason, and rationality. And although we can find an exception to just about every rule in life, the rules we propose should work in the vast majority of circumstances. Beyond this, they must be slightly progressive, as we haven't advanced as a society by retaining all the ignorant ideas of our ancestors. Lastly, they need to have withstood the crucible that is time.

The lessons of history and the inspirational players within it have so much to teach us, if we would only listen and incorporate their knowledge into our daily lives. As historian Will Durant so eloquently put it, "We can not live long in that celestial realm of genius without becoming a little finer than we were, and although we should not find the delirium of youth, we shall know a lasting gentle happiness, a profound delight which time can not take from us until it takes all." All the wisdom we could ever desire is at our fingertips; we only need to pay heed. But, as Marcel Proust observed, "We do not receive wisdom, we must discover it for ourselves after a journey through the wilderness which no one else can make for us, which no one can spare us. For our wisdom is the point of view from which we come at last to regard the world." In other words, parents, school, history, your friends, and this book can lead us to water, but we must realize we're thirsty and do some drinking.

Many go through life proclaiming their faith to a dogmatic religion, thankfully ignoring most of the barbaric ridiculousness contained within its precepts. Some aimlessly search for meaning and fulfillment only to be overwhelmed and undermined by the quantity of information available.

Others despair of the project altogether for lack of results and "lead lives of quiet desperation," as Thoreau so astutely observed. But discovering many of the wonderful possibilities that abound in this life can be realized. With the proper tools, ceaseless effort, and a bit of luck, we can all lead a life of meaning, influence, and achievement.

Why not learn those tools from the most influential teachers? Why struggle with problems that have already been solved? The key component here, of course, is you. You must take action. You must challenge yourself to grow mentally, emotionally, physically, and spiritually.

One of the worst things in life, other than mustard and opera music, is regret and I want you to leave your regret behind forever. I don't want you to wake up one day with the sudden realization that your life has passed you by and that you didn't make the most of all the opportunities you've been given.

This book will help you get there. It is by no means a complete set of rules to live by, and there are other aspects of life that deserve your time and effort. As Bruce Lee said, "Absorb what is useful, discard what is not, add what is uniquely your own." Some of these rules will serve you better than others, but each can truly transform your life if implemented. Let me repeat: if implemented. Understand that knowing is not enough; you must ruthlessly hold yourself accountable and truly live these lessons.

I've come to find, as many do, that life is complicated. But I've also discovered that your philosophy towards it needn't be. One of my aims with this book is not to cheapen these timeless and irreplaceable lessons, but to present them parsimoniously. There is beauty in simplicity, and my goal is to elucidate the power and utility of each as efficiently as I know how. These ideas have been amalgamated through my personal experience and studies, I do not live them perfectly, but I do my best to live them more fully each and every day.

Most of the ideas presented here are not new, or even mine. The only credit I'm willing to take is for the organization, presentation, and the original ideas contained within the bounds of this book. Please trust that I will do my utmost to ensure that credit is given where credit is due.

Furthermore, I am not a doctor, psychologist, or psychiatrist, so these ideas must be vetted at your own risk. No one saves us but ourselves.

In summation, this book is a foundational framework for who you should be on a daily basis. It is a set of ten ideas that work together and build upon each other in order for you to lead a more abundant, fulfilling, and meaningful life. These commandments represent ten of humanity's best ideas.

I hope you find them useful, and I hope they help on your journey to discovering meaning and purpose. I know that if you savor them and incorporate them into your life, they will help. I know without a doubt that they are A Better Ten Commandments.

James Miller

2017

BE THE BEST VERSION OF THYSELF

I

"As human beings, our greatness lies not so much in being able to remake the world … as in being able to remake ourselves."
~ Mahatma Gandhi

"Don't compare yourself with anyone in this world ... if you do so, you are insulting yourself."
~ Bill Gates

"We have no power over external things, and the good that ought to be the object of our earnest pursuit, is to be found only within ourselves."
~ Epictetus

"Look within, for within is the wellspring of virtue, which will not cease flowing, if you cease not from digging."
~ Marcus Aurelius

"There is nothing noble in being superior to your fellow man; true nobility is being superior to your former self."
~ Ernest Hemingway

This rule is your prime directive. This rule is your most important goal. The one thing you should strive for most in life. This is, of course, assuming you have survival down. If you're struggling with food, shelter, and water, then, by all means, let those take precedence. Saving that, raising your standards and holding yourself accountable to being the best version of yourself must be your top priority.

Ask yourself; can I be better at everything I do? Can I be more generous, more grateful, more loving? Can I be a better father or husband, mother or wife, son or daughter, friend or role model? Can I work harder, get smarter, and achieve more? Of course you can. We can all be better at everything we do. All it takes is knowledge from the best and brightest and implementation through the formation of new habits.

Of course, no rule is perfect, so I must insist on a few caveats. If being the best version of yourself includes unethical or unsustainable behaviors, this rule doesn't really pan out. If the parties involved are non-consenting or old enough to so do intelligently (or, let's say, you're a psychopath), this rule is not for you. There are people in this world that are exceptionally good at being bad. Anyone who's visited a psychiatric ward will attest that we are capable of some very depraved mental states. Let's call it "the Jeffery Dahmer exception." After all, when he was asked by authorities why he had preserved seven of his victims' skulls in order to build an altar from which he believed he could derive power, he said he did it for himself: "It was a place where I could feel at home." We can safely say that just because you're good at something, it doesn't make it right. Let us agree that becoming the best version of yourself should fall within the realm of human decency and ethical behavior.

So what do we strive for, to what standards do we hold ourselves accountable? For starters, the other nine commandments contained in this book, but this rule is specifically about what's important to you. It's about who you want to be on a daily basis, it's about discovering the values you hold dear, and it's about what you want to achieve. Do you want to help raise people out of poverty? Do you want to bring joy to others through your art? How about inspiring people to become leaders in their communities? There are endless ways in which you can have an impact. You must ask and answer with clarity, who do you want to be and what do you want to accomplish in this life? As Mark Twain said, "The two most important days in your life are the day you were born, and the day you find out why."

I'm not going to lie to you and say you can do or be anything you want, as there are limits to our abilities – physically, mentally, spiritually, scientifically, etc. At the moment, I can't divine another person's thoughts; we don't know if there's an afterlife; according to physics as we understand it, nothing with mass can travel faster than light; and we can't successfully regenerate lost appendages. But that doesn't mean we can't answer those questions, or at the very least try. (Cool side note, people are currently using frogs and other species to try and regenerate appendages and making some amazing advances in limb regeneration.)

Far too often we sell ourselves too short and severely underestimate what we are capable of achieving. Do you think any successful person ever got where they are by thinking they couldn't achieve their goals? Do you think breakthroughs in technology and medicine occur by people saying, "That's not possible." Of course not. We need not delude ourselves, but by simply believing in the possibility of change, we create a sense of hope rather than despair.

Let's say you had the option to place a limit on how much you could achieve. If that were truly the case, would you? Would you intentionally limit what you could get out of life? Of course not, but we seem to do just that; we talk ourselves into believing that certain things aren't possible for us to achieve. We unwittingly sabotage our very own future and fulfillment.

So how do we move beyond these self-imposed limitations? One of the best ways is to only be in a race with yourself. Stop comparing your results to others; their results are irrelevant, remember your job is to be the best version of yourself, not to be better than anyone else. You are not anyone else, nor will you ever be, so it makes sense that the only person you should try to be better than is the person you were the day before. As Sean Stephenson says in a wonderful TED talk, "I'm only an expert on one thing, and that's how to be me. And I do it well."

If you consistently strive to improve yourself, you always win, and the glory of it all is that you have no idea just how far you can go. As Warren Buffet said, "The best investment you can make is in yourself." Doesn't that sound better than "I can't do that," and "That's not possible?" Furthermore, if self-improvement seems a daunting task, just remember that you're only one decision away from making the right one.

Obviously, circumstances are a factor to be considered when attempting self-improvement. Life for some can be incredibly difficult, and often through no fault of their own. We do not all have the same heredity, the same privileges, the same education, or the same skills, but most of these things can be overcome. Some of the most successful people and world-changing ideas have come from unexpected places.

Take Michael Faraday as an example. You may not know of him, but you almost certainly benefit from his existence, as he invented the electric motor and generator. He also provided the fundamental building blocks for James Clark Maxwell's work on electromagnetic field theory amongst a litany of other achievements in electrical theory and chemistry. Faraday was born to a blacksmiths apprentice in a small town, and his father moved the family to London to find work. His father was frequently sick, and they were often destitute and struggling to feed themselves. Faraday received the most basic of education, learning to read and write through his church. At fourteen, he started delivering newspapers for a book dealer and binder and began reading. Through that reading, he discovered his fascination with electricity and began to study and experiment. Because of that desire to learn and never giving up, if you own anything that uses electricity, you owe Mr. Faraday a debt of gratitude.

Another wonderful example of becoming the best version of yourself is a woman born to a single teenage housemaid in rural Mississippi. That mother left her daughter for work until she was six. Under a destitute grandmother's care, she often wore potato sacks for lack of proper clothing and was ridiculed by other children. At nine she was molested several times by family members and a family friend. At thirteen she ran away from home. At fourteen she got pregnant but lost the child to miscarriage. What is this woman's future? Well, that woman is worth over three billion dollars now, changed countless lives, and her name is Oprah. Of course, there are plenty of other examples: JK Rowling, Sam Walton, Richard Branson, Andrew Carnegie, John D. Rockefeller, and Jim Carrey to name but a few. These individuals are living proof that you can transcend many of your circumstances.

I'd like to touch on accountability for a moment. As a society, we've developed systems that hold people accountable in particular ways: the IRS, the military, the police, the government, etc. When you're a child, you have family, friends, teachers, and mentors. But the most important type of accountability is to yourself. Possessing an unwavering dedication to being an ethical person and having a bondage to one's virtues.

That unwavering dedication reminds me of a parable about a married man who becomes stranded on a deserted island with a beautiful bachelorette. After reaching the conclusion that rescue is not possible, the beautiful woman propositions the man to sleep with her, that they may at least enjoy what little time remains. He responds, "I can't." Perplexed by his response, the woman asks, "Why not; no one will know." His reply, "I'd know." As the Buddha said, "No one saves us but ourselves. No one can and no one may. We ourselves must walk the path."

On your journey to becoming the best version of yourself take care to avoid our innate tendency to be a hypocrite. Most of us love to offer wisdom that we ourselves do not follow. We are typically quite good at recognizing the faults of others, but tend to have a rosy picture of ourselves, hence why the Bible says, "You hypocrite, first take the plank out of your own eye, and then you will see clearly to remove the speck from your brother's."

One reason this is such a glorious piece of wisdom is that our empathy can fail us, especially if we ourselves have not experienced a particular kind of suffering. Think of Dick Cheney changing his stance on homosexuality when he had a gay daughter, or FDR realizing we had to be involved in WWII after his long stance of isolationism. This is why the great philosopher T. Petty said, "You don't know how it feels, you don't know how it feels, no you don't know how it feels, to be me."

Patience should be mentioned here, and will be mentioned again. I have to stress that becoming the best version of yourself takes time. Bill Gates and Warren Buffett didn't get rich overnight. The wisdom of the Buddha or the Bible, Aristotle or Aurelius, wasn't born out of a moment of clarity. Smallpox wasn't cured or penicillin created at the drop of a hat. These things take time, and a wonderful philosophy was expounded on this matter by billionaire Charlie Munger when he stated, "Spend each day trying to be a little bit wiser than you were when you woke up, discharge your duties faithfully and well. Step by step you get ahead but not necessarily in fast spurts... slug it out day by day, inch by inch, if you live long enough most people get what they deserve."

You, yes you, are in the envious position of standing on the shoulders of giants. This is the greatest time in human history to create the life that you want. But remember, life doesn't respond to wants or needs; as Warren Buffets billionaire business partner Charlie Munger said, it responds to deserve.

By implementing the wisdom of heroes and teachers from the past, you can rise above the person you otherwise would have been. By utilizing their lessons and not repeating their mistakes, you can spare yourself much of the unnecessary struggles associated with finding fulfillment. The work, however, is a given; do not delude yourself into thinking that accomplishment comes without effort.

So what does becoming the best version of yourself look like? The capitalistic world of the media and society would have you believe that it's being wealthy and having lots of stuff – a faster car, a bigger bank account, and a mansion on the hill. Unfortunately, these vices typically only bring avarice and worry. Don't get me wrong, money is an excellent tool and allows an incredible amount of freedom, but you must control the money and not let it control you. As Solomon suggests in the Bible, money makes a wonderful servant, but a terrible master.

Possessions, wealth, and lifestyle are also subject to the adaptation principle, where the excitement of a new level is intoxicating for a short while, but eventually becomes the new normal, also known as the hedonic treadmill. You can keep increasing the speed, but unfortunately, you'll never get anywhere. Several interesting studies have shown that lottery winners typically end up right back where they began, returning to their average level of happiness. Others show accident victims regaining their aggregate level of happiness as well, with some even exceeding their pre-accident levels of happiness.

Jim Carrey put it best when he said, "I think everybody should get rich and famous and do everything they ever dreamed of so they can see that it's not the answer." Therefore, I'm much more a fan of John Wooden's definition of success, which is, "The peace of mind attained only through self-satisfaction and knowing you made the effort to do the best of which you're capable."

I imagine you have dreams and desires, things you've always wanted out of life. Well, guess what: they'll never happen if you don't act. Ralph Waldo Emerson said it best, "An ounce of action is worth a ton of theory."

This commandment is about discovering who you are and what you will stand for. It is not about vanity or being selfish, but cultivating your highest virtues. The most valuable things in life are to enjoy every precious moment, to discover your purpose, and to share that gift with the world.

Truly, "No one save us but ourselves."

~ Buddha

DISCOVER SERENITY

II

"Nature knows no pause in progress and development, and attaches her curse on all inaction."

~ Johann Wolfgang von Goethe

"We can not always choose our external circumstances, but we can always choose how to respond to them."

~ Epictetus

"Don't find fault, find a remedy."

~ Henry Ford

"There is never any need to get worked up or to trouble your soul about things you can't control. These things are not asking to be judged by you. Leave them alone."

~ Marcus Aurelius

"To complain is always non-acceptance of what is."

~ Eckhart Tolle

This is the primary rule that governs how you will interact with the vast majority of situations you'll encounter in life. Just about everything that happens to you presents an opportunity to do what is necessary to improve the situation itself or your reaction to that situation. This rule obviously bears a great resemblance to the serenity prayer, which states: God, give me grace to accept with serenity the things that can not be changed, courage to change the things which should be changed, and the wisdom to distinguish the one from the other. But this rule differs in one crucial way, it differs in that this great responsibility isn't bestowed upon or granted to you by some higher power. As the Epictetus quote above suggests, it's something you must strive for and achieve for yourself. Simply put yourself in gods shoes, and attempt to understand the balance between taking action or choosing acceptance.

The first part of this rule is all about what you control, the things on which you can have a direct and discernible impact; your attitude, your career, your friends, your income, your ethics, your words, and everything else you choose. Everything that happens to you, ask yourself, "Can I do something about this? Can I make this situation better? Can I provide a solution?" When the answer is yes, it's your job and no one else's to enact those answers.

Most people let things go unsaid; most people let bad scenarios develop by standing idly by. Don't be like most people. You should take the initiative to tackle your problems head-on. This isn't about making people uncomfortable or just to stir the pot, but to make the best of every situation you encounter. Enacting this part of the rule is about doing what needs to be done and saying what needs to be said.

Understanding how effective your actions are is a crucial element in this rule. You don't want your efforts to worsen whatever situation you find yourself in, or to be a waste of your most precious resource, your time. If effectively deployed, your choices will have an enormous positive impact on your life, your relationships, and on the world in which we live.

When employing this method, remember to avoid the lottery mentality, thinking that success or change should come overnight. That is not how the world typically works. Big achievements and changes take consistent daily practice. As Lao-Tzu said, "A journey of a thousand miles must begin with a single step," and I like to add that you must ensure that you're stepping in the right direction. The best place to start, of course, is with yourself, hence why being the best version of yourself is the first commandment. As Gandhi said, "Be the change you want to see in the world."

Most of us want to have an impact; most of us want to be relevant. We want to leave a legacy, and we spend much of our time offering sage advice to others that we ourselves do not follow. But talk is cheap, it is our actions that will truly have an impact and show the wisdom of our ways. We must lead by example, we must talk less and do more, and we must hold ourselves accountable to our values.

Of course, we must add a few caveats, such as differentiating between "should" and "can." Just because you can do something, it doesn't make it right. This is where we must rely on the other commandments. Is the act loving? Does it conform to the golden rule? Does it provide perspective? Will everyone involved be grateful in the long run? Does it come from a place of compassion? Does it encourage growth? When you bring all these commandments together, it provides a framework for the type of action you should be taking when you have the power to influence the situation.

That being said, there is an endless list of things in life you can't change. For example: to whom you were born, when and where you were born, your genetic code, what the weather will be like next Tuesday, what you regret having done last Thursday, what happened to you in 1987, what's going to happen in twenty-seven minutes, your left knee hurting, getting old, dying, the boiling point of molybdenum (~8382 F if you're curious), and the traumatic memory of seeing your grandfather naked when you were twelve (we called him "the creeper" for a multitude of reasons, and he was the spitting image of Mr. Burns from *The Simpsons,* so you can imagine the despair).

We tend to spend a great deal of time worrying about many of these things (save the molybdenum, of course), but who wants to lead a life full of stress and anxiety worrying about things you can't change? Wouldn't you rather lead a life of acceptance of these unchangeable aspects of your existence – a life lived in peace with these immutable truths? This can be achieved simply through a change in attitude and an awareness of what you have control over and that which you do not. Time is your most valuable resource, and you can never get more, so why waste it fretting about the aspects of life over which you exert no control?

We all have an inkling that life is what happens when you're busy making other plans, as Yogi Berra said, "It's tough to make predictions, especially about the future." Knowing this, it's not what happens in life, but rather how we react to life that matters most. Don't make excuses, don't blame the world, and don't baselessly rationalize your current reality. Learn to live this commandment, as your ability to adapt to all the adversity that life can throw at you has a direct impact on your level of contentment. As Albert Einstein said, "The measure of intelligence is the ability to change."

There are endless ways in which life can be unfair, and I hate to be the bearer of bad news, but it would seem that nature has no compulsion to take care of us. As the pessimist would say, if you don't work at life, it automatically works against you. There is a very long list of things trying to kill you in this world, and if you don't believe me, just walk out into the wilderness without any of the wonderful technological advancements we've come to take for granted, and try to feed and shelter yourself. I promise you'll quickly be humbled.

Tragedies abound every moment of every day in every far-flung part of the globe. For instance, it is estimated that over 99 percent of all the species that have ever graced this planet are extinct. Or look at the infant mortality rate for children under the age of five. As of 2012, 6.6 million die every year; that's over 18,000 a day, over 750 an hour, and just over 12.5 a minute. That's down from 12.7 million per year in 1990. The progress made hasn't happened through the power of prayer, faith, miracles or conversion; this has happened through improvements in technology, science and medicine, the spreading of education to the developing world, and through the actions of organizations like UNICEF, OXFAM, and Doctors Without Borders.

These organizations live the first part of this commandment. Are they perfect? Of course not, but they're putting in the effort and taking action to spread social justice throughout the world. This is the critical distinction made earlier between Epictetus' accounting of the rule and the serenity prayer. This places the burden upon each of us to make the world a better place, to take action and get involved, not to pass the buck to a higher power when nature shows you the unjust side of reality.

So how do we tell the difference between what is within our power to change and what we must accept? Obviously, there is a vast continuum in the amount of influence we can have on a particular issue, ranging from zero to complete control and everything in between. The short answer is education. Through mentors in life and print, sustained study, and implementation of lessons learned, you can drastically improve your ability to differentiate between the necessary course of either action or acceptance.

When problems are massive in scale such as the ever-present battles to bring global, cultural, social, societal, and political change, we can quickly become overwhelmed and apathetic by the seeming inadequacy of our efforts. Societies and governments are vast and complex machines with an innumerable amount of moving parts, and just as large freight ships do not turn on a dime, social, cultural, and political progress takes time.

Just because change is slow, mutiny is rarely warranted, as we all know breaking things is much easier than rebuilding them. One must take the view of Martin Luther King Jr. when he said, "The arc of the moral universe is long, but it bends towards justice." To which I must add, as long as we do our part. If you're familiar with history, you'll understand just how easy it is for a society to slip from the ever-upward slope of progress. Two Edmund Burke quotes come to mind regarding this concept, "Those that don't know history are destined to repeat it," and, "The only thing necessary for the triumph of evil is for good men to do nothing."

Opposite the large end of the spectrum, we have smaller scale issues, such as a personal problem that demands our attention and we ignore to our own detriment, or a minor inconvenience that we magnify to a level of absurdity that's completely unwarranted. Most have simple solutions, but for lack of knowledge or effort in the former case, or perspective and emotional intelligence in the latter, people struggle with these petty issues daily, weekly, monthly, yearly, and unfortunately for many, over the course of an entire lifetime.

The solution to our problems, both minuscule and monstrous, is learning to live this commandment each and every moment of one's life. Anything that happens in life, we decide how to respond. As I stated in the opening of this chapter, every interaction, every event, every waking second is an opportunity. Whether it's tragedy or trauma, heartbreak or loss, a petty grievance or an ill-spoken word, every moment is an opportunity for us to grow emotionally, strengthen the bonds that connect us to others, and accept all that comes our way in this incredible life.

A quote often attributed to Viktor Frankl comes to mind, "Between stimulus and response there's a space. In that space lies our power to choose our response. In our response lies our growth and our happiness."

LOVE SELFLESSLY

III

"Our duty is to encourage every one in his struggle to live up to his own highest idea, and strive at the same time to make the ideal as near as possible to the Truth."

~ *Swami Vivekananda*

"It is more blessed to give than receive."

~ *Jesus*

"We make a living by what we get. We make a life by what we give."

~ *Winston Churchill*

"Only a life lived for others is the life worth while."

~ *Albert Einstein*

"No one is useless in this world who lightens the burdens of another."

~ *Charles Dickens*

The first two commandments in this book form the basis of how we interact with ourselves. The current and subsequent commandments will guide our thinking in how we interact with others. They will form the foundation of our relationships with friends, family, and even strangers. As you can see from the quotations above, in its most simplistic form, my definition of love is to help others become the best version of themselves. In life, once we've discovered our gifts and live our better nature, it is our duty to help others do the same.

Romantic love and sex, both wonderful in their own right, are undoubtedly part of a well-balanced and well-lived life, but the kind of love discussed in this chapter is the love we'd wish to receive from every non-romantic or non-sexual interaction from our fellow brothers and sisters. It's the kind of love that the Buddha spoke of when he said, "Radiate boundless love towards the entire world, above, below and across, unhindered, without ill will, without enmity." The type of love I'm speaking of is platonic and given with no expectations. This type of love is selfless, not transactional. And the true wonder and beauty of this type of love is that if you expect nothing, then everything given you will truly be a blessing.

Obviously, there is a long list of barriers to accomplishing this end; selfishness, racism, tribalism, and nationalism are but a few. I'd also add religion to that list, as at the root of every belief system is in-group and out-group thinking. Religion by its very nature is inherently divisive, and there's an endless list of human conflicts that adequately prove my point. All of the good that religion claims responsibility for (community, charity, spirituality, ethics, etc.) needn't be beholden to a specific faith, for all of these wonderful aspects of life can be experienced and lived regardless of which faith you practice or without believing anything at all. As the late Christopher Hitchens was fond of saying, "Name one ethical statement made, or one ethical action performed, by a believer that could not have been uttered or done by a nonbeliever."

Obviously, religions do provide a means for ethical acts, but it is in our nature to do good works, and therefore religion is not their cause. To a certain extent, we are by nature fundamentally good. Furthermore, ask yourself which is better: doing an ethical act because you think the creator of the universe will reward you for it, or simply doing it for the act itself?

I want to keep the forms of selfless love that are spoken of in our holy books. I want to encourage the boundless love of Buddhism, the Zakat of Islam, the donations to the poor from the fields of the Israelites, and the parable of the good Samaritan. But I also realize that all of these forms of love operate on their own merit. I've had the glorious opportunity to witness human decency from a multitude of nationalities, ethnicities, and faiths, and it's obvious to me that our benevolence and ethical intuitions run far deeper than any border or belief system.

Religions are some of our very first attempts at understanding our reality. They are some of the very first attempts at organizing and building a society. They are an attempt at forming human solidarity. But being that they are some of the earliest ideas, they are invariably some of the worst. Though some of the sagest wisdom has come from our earliest history, some of the most atrocious advice has as well. This book, therefore, is an attempt to "winnow the wheat from the chaff" as it were.

By disregarding the errors of our ancestors, and in the absence of faith, how will we form a durable and just civilization? A human solidarity that promotes the general welfare should obviously be the ultimate goal. We must realize that whether we like it or not, we are all in this together, and we need to learn ways of creating and maintaining a more prosperous, fulfilling, and fair existence. Of course, there are dangerous elements of human solidarity that need to be considered; North Korea is practicing a particular form, but it would seem as though the general welfare of its citizenry is low on the nation's priority list. The Nazis had their own form of solidarity as well, but with an obviously perverse sense of what it meant to be human.

The kind of human solidarity of which I speak was on display when Bruce Lee was asked if he thought of himself as Chinese or American, and his response was perfect. He stated that he thought of himself as a human being. Whether we like it or not, we are all in this game of life together. We must do all that we can to get along with one another. We must do everything in our power to make the most of our lives. We must do everything we can to protect and preserve this precious planet we call home.

Part of the beauty of life is certainly all the wonderful diversity and uniqueness in our cultures, languages, and histories, but it's what we all have in common that brings us together and helps promote a durable and desirable future. No matter the faith or politics, the country or continent; at our very core, we share far more than that which differentiates us from one another. In the end, we all want the same thing: a life lived with a maximum of fulfillment and a minimum of suffering. The conflict only arises when we disagree on how to attain that end.

Why is loving selflessly such a difficult task, and is it even worth the effort? Many of the most rewarding events in one's life come after a protracted effort, through struggles and sacrifice or emotional and physical discomfort. Would life be as enjoyable if we didn't occasionally fail? Would it be as rewarding if success required no toil, no strain? Many books and movies would have us believe that once you can afford to sip cocktails on the beach all day long, then you've won the race. But anyone who's tried it will tell you that it's only satisfying for a short time and better enjoyed as a reward. After a few days of doing nothing, you will soon find yourself bored and searching for something on which to focus your attention. This is one of the reasons non-transactional love can be so rewarding. It forces us to be selfless, to sacrifice our time and interests for another. It has us choose forgiveness rather than retaliation, community over rivalry, and to give rather than take. Instead of choosing the path of least resistance, love encourages the hard choices. Love by its very nature is its own reward. It is the ultimate gift.

The most basic and obvious purpose of life is certainly survival, and for the time being, we seem to have managed that task well enough (many would argue far too well). Unfortunately, some of the traits critical to survival directly oppose and impede our capacity to selflessly love one another and achieve the goal of maximum fulfillment and minimum suffering. Competition, aggression, and deeming hierarchical status are still useful tools socially, politically, and economically, but they need to be subdued in order for us to cooperate and progress in a more earnest manner. I'm under no illusion that these traits are not critical to our society, nor am I by any means a pacifist. I realize there is still a necessary and just use for competition, aggression, status, and even violence. Speaking only of violence, there are people in this world that aren't interested in creating a durable future for humanity, whether through ideology, indoctrination, or psychosis; some individuals only want to see this world fail. If these people aren't open to dialogue, then there is but one option: their removal from society through force. There is hope, however, that as we grow as a society, violence will become less and less of a necessity.

Beyond our mere survival, we must endeavor to create a common purpose that promotes human fulfillment and relieves human suffering, a common purpose that is more egalitarian and sustainable and transcends national, racial, economic, tribal, religious, ethnic, and cultural identities. Love will most certainly be a crucial element in that common purpose. We must ask and answer honestly, honorably, and justly how we would wish this world to be. As individuals and as a society, we must make a concerted effort to promote humanity's best ideas and encourage a human solidarity that is both reasonable and ethical. Although a very modest one indeed, this book represents such an effort.

How does one practice this commandment? One method is through prohibition, and the Jain patriarch Mahavira put it about as well as it can be said, “Do not injure, abuse, oppress, enslave, insult, torment, torture, or kill any creature or living being.” This is a wonderful start, but there are obviously necessary actions other than prohibition to partake in as well. We practice love through the act of bringing people together and making the most of our gifts and abilities. We’ve already touched on many of these elements, but the following is a short list of ways to serve: forgiveness, compassion, philanthropy, thoughtfulness, honesty, support, recognition, sacrifice, kindness, gratitude, mentorship, sympathy, generosity, aid, enthusiasm, music, comedy, education, etc.

Some of us are better suited than others at each of the aforementioned skills, but you need not perfect or practice them all; pick a few and go make the world a more joyful, inviting, and loving place. As the Dickens quote said, “No one is useless in this world who lightens the burdens of another.”

PRACTICE POSITIVE RECIPROCITY

IV

"Zigong asked, 'Is there one word that can serve as a principle of conduct for life?' Confucius replied it is the word reciprocity. Do not impose on others what you yourself do not desire."

~ *Confucius*

"Love your neighbor as yourself."

~ *Leviticus*

"Hence, by self-control and by making *dharma* (right conduct) your main focus, treat others as you treat yourself."

~*Mahbhrata Shanti-Parva*

"What thou avoidest suffering thyself, seek not to impose on others."

~ *Epictetus*

"Treat your inferior as you would wish your superior to treat you."

~ *Seneca*

This is probably the closest thing to a moral imperative that humanity has ever discovered. Emanating from Egypt, Babylon, Greece, Rome, Persia, China, and India, reciprocity is one of the most commonly touted ethics in religious and moral texts. Not only does it work in the positive form, "Do unto others as you'd do unto yourself," it also works in the negative, "Do not impose on others what you yourself do not desire." A version of this adage can be found in: The Analects of Confucius, Greek and Roman philosophy, the religious texts of Judaism, Christianity, Zoroastrianism, Taoism, Maoism, Buddhism, Hinduism, Sikhism, Jainism, Islam, and my personal favorite Scientology (how ridiculous are those people ... hail to our galactic overlord Xenu. I mean come on folks. Hubbard was a professional science fiction writer for fuck's sake!).

Its earliest textual representation appears to come from an ancient Egyptian story called "The elegant peasant," in which the peasant pleads to have a wrong righted by stating, "Now this is the command: do to the doer to cause that he do." Like the flood stories of Ziusudra, Gilgamesh, and Atrahasis turned into Noah's flood, or the book of Proverbs borrowed from Egypt's Instructions of Amenemope, it's very suggestive that the Israelites adapted their version of this timeless axiom from the Egyptians, Sumerians, and Babylonians. But regardless of who thought of it first, if applied in the right way, it's a wonderful moral precept.

We must differentiate between the three commonly used forms of reciprocity, but recognize that they are all versions of the same thing. In the earliest forms, it's to be used as a punishment, "do to the doer." It then turns into a means of ethical conduct through either action or prohibition by considering how you'd treat yourself.

As with just about every rule though, we can find exceptions. People that enjoy pain or discomfort themselves, known as masochists, probably shouldn't utilize reciprocity too liberally or often. In its crudest form, stemming from the Egyptian text previously mentioned, the Babylonian Hammurabi's Code, and repeated in the Talmud and Old Testament, most of us are familiar with the expression "an eye for an eye and a tooth for a tooth." But there are certain forms of reciprocity that should be denied, as when accidents occur. For instance, say a parent inadvertently runs over their child backing out of the driveway; should they be killed as well? Jesus was reported to have said that an eye for an eye was the old way and to turn the other cheek, but forgiveness isn't always warranted either. Some individuals are irredeemable and must be forcibly removed from society, such as serial killers unwilling to see the value of a civil society and modernity.

We also must take into consideration short-term versus long-term effects. Take a supposedly innocent white lie said to avoid immediate discomfort. A friend asks if you think they should lose a few pounds, and to avoid hurting their feelings, you say they look fine. But what does your friend truly want; honesty and health, or a lie to avoid momentary discomfort? Furthermore, not everyone has the same desires, so reciprocity doesn't work as a catch-all, but given a few caveats, it does form a sound foundation from which to begin many personal interactions.

I'd like to touch on the origins of reciprocity for a moment, as most people would tend to think this is a distinctly human trait, but evidence abounds in the animal kingdom. Take the vampire bats mentioned in the introduction. After a night of feeding, a successful bat will regurgitate and provide blood to an unsuccessful bat. They will share more readily with related bats (kin altruism) and those that have previously shared with them (tit for tat). There are even asshole bats that ask for a loan and then don't return the favor. Kin altruism explains and justifies sacrifices made for family members that ensure the survival of familial genes. The tit for tat strategy, where by animals help unrelated members who previously helped them, and refuse to help those unwilling to share the burden of responsibility, is a form of reciprocal altruism that justifies the sacrifice of the individual for the group's survival. More examples, you ask? Interspecies cleaning, egg trading, and predator inspection in fish, egg protection and alarm calling in birds, non-kin parenting in carnivores, midwifery in bats, social grooming in primates, and food sharing in chimps, are just a few examples.

We, of course, differ in many ways from any other species on the planet, but we share far more in common with the animal kingdom than many care to admit. Reciprocity is just one glaring example of that commonality. So is our reciprocity any different? I would say that the tools and tactics used are more complex, but the root mechanism is exactly the same. I would also argue that the critical difference is that we can exercise far more choice in how we respond to a given situation. Hence why I say practice positive reciprocity. For just as bad begets bad, good begets good.

When we reciprocate insult for insult or blow for blow, we enter an escalating trend of division and distrust, or worse yet, hate and violence. This commandment is about being the bigger person and ending the escalation through our actions. We can choose not to engage in negative reciprocity, we can use the art of persuasion to dissuade our malefactor, or if necessary, the use of minimal force. You are not the instigator or provocateur; you are the solution.

Another way our reciprocity is different is that we are one of a few ultra-social species on the planet. By all being related, ants, bees, wasps, and termites managed this feat through the mechanism of kin altruism. Our ultra-sociality, however, is built upon communication, cooperation, and sharing, allowing us to form alliances with unrelated peers. Other mammals communicate and form cooperative groups, but our alliances are far more strategic, complex, vaster, and involve different cognitive processes.

So just how useful is positive reciprocity? Well, for starters, it's obviously the rule mentioned in the introduction that can replace commandments five through nine in one fell swoop. Would you prefer to not be respected by your children, how about murdered, stolen from, cheated on, or lied about? The wonderful thing though, is that this rule doesn't just work for commandments five through nine; it also works for other major ethical violations. Should we practice abuse, slavery, or torture? How about human trafficking or forced prostitution? It also works on minor issues such as a smile, opening a door, or returning a lost wallet. I want to be loved and treated with respect, therefore I treat others the same way. When I ask someone a question, I want an honest answer, so I don't lie. I willingly do favors, as I hope someone would do the same for me. This rule works in so many situations it's uncanny.

Many of us have a tendency to only practice positive reciprocity with kin and those in our immediate circle of influence, and some even have a hard time doing that much. Many more give the remainder of those we interact with lip service, and some go even further and avoid everyday interactions altogether. The message in the parable of the Good Samaritan is instructive here, in that it shows us that anyone, even those outside the in-group, can be our "neighbor."

There's another elephant in the room that must be addressed, and that is the ever-pervasive mentality of "what's in it for me?" Of course, this is caused by our natural tendency to be more selfish than cooperative, and it makes evolutionary sense. We must feed, protect, and nurture ourselves and kin before we can assist another, otherwise we'd never survive.

But if you can flip this script and offer before you ask, you can immediately improve every relationship you have. Implementing this simple principle will open doors and show you opportunities you never would have thought possible. Living this rule will have a profound and long-lasting impact on every aspect of your life.

In summation, given my caveats, we should treat everyone with dignity and respect. We should offer before we ask, and we should always practice a positive reciprocity. Think of all the brief interactions you have on a daily basis that could be more meaningful and authentic. Going about your day, ask yourself how you can be a better representative of one of humanity's best qualities. Learn to be an exemplar of this wonderful tenet of human nature and push people's reciprocity reflex for the right reasons. It will strengthen the bonds you form with others and create far more meaningful relationships. I implore you, go out and give. Give, and give some more, and I promise, you shall receive.

FIND PERSPECTIVE

V

"What we are today comes from our thoughts of yesterday, and our present thoughts build our life of tomorrow: Our life is the creation of our mind."

~ ***Buddha***

"The whole world is change, life is but what you deem it."

~ ***Marcus Aurelius***

"It's not what you look at that matters, it's what you see."

~ ***Henry David Thoreau***

"The man who is truly good and wise will bear with dignity whatever fortune sends and will always make the best of his circumstances."

~ ***Aristotle***

"There is nothing either good or bad, but thinking makes it so."

~ ***William Shakespeare***

Could things be worse? This is a rhetorical question of course. and a great one to ask yourself anytime you're in the midst of an undesirable situation. We can use questions like this or creative thoughts as levers to pry our minds out of our present suffering. As the Buddha suggests, "The mind is the source of happiness and unhappiness by what it chooses to compare the experience with. If it chooses to compare it to something worse, then it will create happiness, gratitude, and pride, but if it chooses to compare it to something better, then it will create unhappiness, bitterness and envy."

This tactic of using thoughts to pry our minds out of our present suffering has a number of approaches. A friend of mine simply asks, "Is there a gun to your head?" Sam Harris speaks of this tactic in *Waking Up* by describing a series of water leaks in his home and subsequently becoming more aggravated with each new deluge. During the fourth such onslaught while "beginning to rage like King Lear in the storm," his wife suggested that they should be thankful that it was freshwater rather than sewage pouring through the ceiling. Using these types of thoughts can be a formidable tool in finding peace whatever your circumstance.

So how much worse could it possibly be? If you read the paper or watch the news, you don't even need to use your imagination. Beyond that, documentaries and statistics are littered with an endless supply of disasters and tragedies. But even if you're the subject or the statistic, it could still be worse. I don't mean to oversimplify and minimize all the human suffering that exists or suggest that you can transcend all the injustice and pain in the world by simply changing your mind. Nor do I propose deluding yourself into accepting all the evil in the world. But for every wrongdoing you don't have the power to change, there is a bright side, and it should be your goal to find it.

We are all subject to our thoughts, and if you can change your thoughts, you can change your world. As author Henry Miller says, "Life has no other discipline to impose, if we would but realize it, than to accept life unquestioningly ... everything we deny, denigrate or despise, serves to defeat us in the end. What seems nasty, painful, evil can become a source of beauty, joy, and strength if faced with an open mind. Every moment is a golden one for him who has the vision to recognize it as such."

Another wonderful tool to find perspective is that of scale, and there's no better place to find it than space. NASA's Voyager 1 space probe and the Hubble space telescope have both taken a multitude of incredible images that everyone on the planet should see, and two, in particular, come to mind.

The first was taken by Hubble and is called "the Ultra-Deep Field." Words won't do it justice, but I'll do my best to describe the image. Beginning in late 2003 and concluding in January of 2004, the Hubble telescope took several long exposures of a miniscule part of the sky that even with our best ground-based telescopes looked barren. The total area observed is approximately 1/13,000,000th of the night sky or a bit smaller than pointing skyward and peering through a straw. The exposures totaled just shy of 1 million seconds or about 11.5 days, and when the images were combined, everyone was astonished by the result.

In this apparently void patch of sky, they found approximately 10000 galaxies, each containing billions upon billions of stars. The light from the faintest objects had been traveling for approximately 13.2 billion years at the speed of light (186,000 miles, or about 7.5 times around the earth, per second) to reach us.

You can't possibly fathom how large the universe is, but let us ponder it for a moment. Let's say you wanted to travel to the closest star other than our sun. How long do you think it would take to get there? (Guess before continuing, or it's no fun.) Of course, this depends on your mode of transport; the space shuttle, for instance, travels at about 17,600 mph, but I'm sorry to say that it's going to take you about 165,000 years to get there.

How about something faster? In 2015, NASA's New Horizon's probe reached a whooping 52,000 mph, but even at that speed, it would take over 54,000 years to reach Proxima Centauri, our nearest solar neighbor. Remember that there are at least 100 billion stars in our galaxy alone and at least 2 trillion galaxies; that's a greater number of stars than there are grains of sand on planet earth...and that's just what we can see so far.

The other image was taken by the Voyager 1 space probe at the request of astronomer Carl Sagan back in 1990. After it had completed its primary mission studying Jupiter, Saturn, and their moons, Sagan suggested turning the craft around to take a photograph of Earth. He opined that the image wouldn't have much scientific value but could be meaningful nonetheless for providing some perspective on our place in the cosmos.

At the time the image was taken, Voyager 1 had passed the orbit of Pluto and was about 3.7 billion miles away. In it, and hardly visible, Earth faintly appears as just 1/12th of a pixel amongst 640,000 awash in a beam of sunlight refracted by the camera lens. I'll let Sagan continue.

> *We succeeded in taking that picture, and, if you look at it, you see a dot. That's here. That's home. That's us. On it, everyone you ever heard of, every human being who ever lived, lived out their lives. The aggregate of all our joys and sufferings, thousands of confident religions, ideologies and economic doctrines, every hunter and forager, every hero and coward, every creator and destroyer of civilizations, every king and peasant, every young couple in love, every hopeful child, every mother and father, every inventor and explorer, every teacher of morals, every corrupt politician, every superstar, every supreme leader, every saint and sinner in the history of our species, lived there – on a mote of dust, suspended in a sunbeam.*
>
> *The Earth is a very small stage in a vast cosmic arena. Think of the rivers of blood spilled by all those generals and emperors so that in*

> *glory and in triumph they could become the momentary masters of a fraction of a dot. Think of the endless cruelties visited by the inhabitants of one corner of the dot on scarcely distinguishable inhabitants of some other corner of the dot. How frequent their misunderstandings, how eager they are to kill one another, how fervent their hatreds. Our posturings, our imagined self-importance, the delusion that we have some privileged position in the universe, are challenged by this point of pale light.*
>
> *[...] To my mind, there is perhaps no better demonstration of the folly of human conceits than this distant image of our tiny world. To me, it underscores our responsibility to deal more kindly and compassionately with one another and to preserve and cherish that pale blue dot, the only home we've ever known.*
>
> *— Carl Sagan, speech at Cornell University, October 13, 1994*

Now that's perspective. I encourage anyone and everyone to find and appreciate these images or any image for that matter that brings the joy of living into the present and encourages you to appreciate your existence.

Another tool at our disposal for finding perspective is cognitive therapy, and if you could sum up the entirety of that particular field in one go, it would be seeing the bright side. Of course, it's far more complex than that, but the bulk of the work consists of identifying certain negative thought patterns and then reappraising and replacing them with more realistic or positive thoughts. You don't even need the couch, the therapist, or an exorbitant bill to do it. Every time you have a negative thought, write it down and seek a way to reappraise it as insignificant or use that thought as an opportunity to learn or grow. For example, I grew up in Utah as a non-Mormon and was regularly ostracized from the in-group, which initially fostered a sense of resentment. I reappraised my attitude toward that time in my life and feel that it made me a much stronger person. I let those negative experiences build my character.

Here's a parable about just how powerful perspective can be. During the course of an interview, a reporter discovered that the successful business owner she was questioning had a brother who ended up in jail. She decided to dig a bit and found that their father was also in jail. Prior to this calamity, the father was single and struggling to make ends meet and was doing everything he could think of just to stay above water. Unfortunately, he couldn't handle the pressure and ended up falling into a life of crime and despair. Eventually, the law caught up with him, and the boys found themselves in separate foster homes. Curious, the reporter wanted to find out what caused the boys to take such divergent paths in life and asked them what they thought made the crucial difference ending up where they did. Astonishingly, they had the same answer. With a father like mine, where else would I be?

Another great way to find perspective is by reading history. As historian Will Durrant said, "Most of us spend too much time on the last twenty-four hours, and too little on the last six thousand years." Consider the brutal, nasty, and brief life of a serf in the Middle Ages, having to live under tyrannical governance and an overbearing and all too willing to kill church. Think of the life of an Egyptian stonemason during the construction of the pyramids, living only as a pawn in a Pharaoh's fantasy. Go back even further and imagine yourself in the late Paleolithic, having to fend off wild animals, living in a cave, and only having a 60 percent chance of making it to age fifteen.

And though the world has unquestioningly advanced in a multitude of ways, irony is still alive and well, generating an incredible amount of present-day suffering. The female genital mutilation community is still alive and well; only 38 percent of people in Afghanistan can read; many people in south-central Asia still live under a caste system with no real chance of transcending their place in society. Even in our modern-day advanced societies, suffering is all around us. The prisons and hospitals, the psych wards and convalescent homes, and of course, that all-important space that sits in between our ears.

If you're lucky enough to be reading this book right now, you're actually in some pretty rarified company. According to a PEW Research report, 71 percent of the world lives on less than ten dollars per day. Most of these people don't have the great privilege of discovering and incorporating these precious rules into their daily habits. I'm not saying that their lives can't be filled with joy and meaning, or that they can't find perspective. I'm just saying that if you have the freedom to read this book, you have more opportunities in life than almost every person that has ever lived.

Perspective is about choosing what we fill our heads with. It's about using psychological tools to reframe how we view the world. It's about keeping ourselves honest and compensating for our propensity to take things for granted. As I said before, good begets good, and your thoughts are no exception. By thinking of all the possible alternatives, we can pry ourselves from our present suffering. Through scale, we can use perspective to realize the true magnitude of a negative event and through reappraisal, we can discover a more positive way of looking at life events. By using all of these tools we create an environment of growth.

When we choose to look at the bright side of life, we create a feedback loop of positivity, and our happiness becomes a self-fulfilling prophecy. As the Buddha says, "We are shaped by our thoughts; we become what we think. When the mind is pure, joy follows like a shadow that never leaves."

BE GRATEFUL

VI

"He is a wise man who does not grieve for the things which he has not, but rejoices for those which he has."

~ ***Epictetus***

"When you arise in the morning, think of what a precious privilege it is to be alive-- to breathe, to think, to enjoy, to love"

~ ***Marcus Aurelius***

"Gratitude is not only the greatest of virtues, but the parent of all others."

~ ***Cicero***

"Let us be grateful to the people who make us happy; they are the charming gardeners who make our souls blossom."

~ ***Marcel Proust***

"Gratitude bestows reverence, allowing us to encounter everyday epiphanies, those transcendent moments of awe that change forever how we experience life and the world."

~ ***John Milton***

I like to tell myself that there is both good and bad in the world and that I get to decide what I look at and support through my thoughts and actions. The world is full of wonders and atrocities, triumphs and tragedies, but it is our mind that is the arbiter of our mental disposition toward these events. Through the practice of perspective, we can realize just how bad it could be, and through the gift of gratitude, we can celebrate how truly wondrous it is. I am of course not suggesting we be irrationally detached from our reality, but ask yourself how dissatisfied do you need to be while attempting to make your life and our world a better place.

As mentioned in the introduction, every trait you possess operates in a continuum of nature and nurture, and happiness is no different. It is a highly heritable trait, and happy parents tend to have happy babies. It is not however set in stone. Gratitude, you'll discover, is one activity in which you can actively engage in order to increase your general level of contentment. It is a wondrous tool that can serve as a wellspring of increasing one's fulfillment in just about every aspect of one's life.

Can you think of any successful people that tend to have a bad attitude? To many, if you ask me. Typically, we don't enjoy the company of such people, for negative attitudes tend to be repulsive. The people we truly enjoy spending the most time around are usually the most grateful and positive. As stated in the chapter on positive reciprocity, good begets good. Gratitude, like love, manifests its own rewards. Just as another person's laughter invokes our own, gratitude is contagious. Since we enjoy the company of positive and grateful people, it certainly makes sense to cultivate those virtues within ourselves.

Think of all things we take for granted on a daily basis. Just taking stock of my current surroundings, there is an endless list of things for which I can be thankful. For example, the computer on which I type this book and the myriad of jobs on which its production lies. The electricity that powers it and the thousands of people that had a hand in creating the knowledge base and structure of providing that electricity. The clothes on my back, the food in my fridge, the roof over my head, the clean water that comes out of the tap, the favors of a friend, and the love of my family. Not to mention the incredible freedom of living in a safe and prosperous country. There are so many things to be thankful for it's quite ridiculous.

When we remind ourselves of all that we have to be grateful for, it elicits a feeling of well-being, and this effect has been studied quite extensively. One such study had three groups of students writing a few sentences once a week. The first group wrote about things they were grateful for, the second about irritations or displeasing events, and the third about events that had no discernible effect positive or negative. After ten weeks, not only did the group writing about positive experiences feel better about their lives and tended to be more optimistic, but they also exercised more and saw the doctor less. Another study surveyed the effects of certain interventions and showed that writing a thank you letter to someone who'd previously performed a favor which hadn't been properly acknowledged showed immediate and long-lasting increases in happiness. So start writing down the things you're grateful for; I promise it will make you happier.

One great hurdle to maximizing our gratitude is a propensity to be natural pessimists, also known as our negativity bias. Our brains are finely tuned for finding bad in the world, and it makes evolutionary sense. Our very survival depends on perceiving threats in the world and reacting quickly to them. Author and neuropsychologist Rick Hanson describes our evolutionary past in terms of playing the ultimate game of carrot (food, sex, cooperation) and stick (death, disease, injury). Obviously, if you miss a few carrots it's not the end of the world, but if you miss a stick, it most likely spells disaster. Not only does your brain perceive negative events more readily, but also more rapidly and more persistently than equivalent positive events. We constantly attempt to assimilate information and categorize situations we hope to avoid in the future. Over the last several hundred thousand years, our lives have drastically changed for the better, but unfortunately, our brains have not. This is one reason we overreact to insignificant events such as an insult or being cut off in traffic; they elicit a similar negative response though they're obviously far more benign. It's also the same reason we find car wrecks, tragic news stories, and smear campaigns so compelling.

How can we combat the negativity bias? Just knowing that you have one helps negate its effects, but there are other ways of compensating as well. The gratitude journal mentioned earlier works wonders. Take the time to write down things you're grateful for, concentrate on people rather than things, and write consistently. Know that it takes longer to recognize and remember positive events; linger on pleasing interactions and occurrences. Have ammunition at the ready, be it a quote, a poem, a short story, or a positive memory. You can also engage in a mentally-taxing activity, which tends to reduce our emotionality. These are all great tools in helping you break free from your inner caveman, thereby preventing him from dragging you down a path paved with suffering.

Not only does gratitude help you overcome your negativity bias, but there are a number of other substantial benefits as well. Authors Eric Mosley and Derek Irvine list fourteen scientifically proven positive aspects of gratitude in the book *The Power of Thanks*. Grateful people are less depressed, healthier, and more resistant to trauma. They also sleep better, have better relationships, and achieve more. They are more giving, content, and engaged. And as suggested before, gratitude creates a feedback loop of both internal and external benefits. Gratitude promotes giving, which causes happiness and improves relationships, which in turn causes more gratitude and giving. In another study, researchers at the University of

Connecticut found that gratitude can even lower your risk of a heart attack. What's not to like?

Obviously, gratitude is one of the highest virtues one can cultivate in one's self. Its benefits are long-lived and overwhelmingly positive, both internally and externally. No matter your circumstance, there are things to be grateful for, and it's worth taking the time to account for them. As the Buddha says, "Let us rise up and be thankful, for if we didn't learn a lot today, at least we learned a little, and if we didn't learn a little, at least we didn't get sick, and if we got sick, at least we didn't die; so, let us all be thankful."

CULTIVATE A RATIONAL COMPASSION

VII

"Our human compassion binds us the one to the other - not in pity or patronizingly, but as human beings who have learnt how to turn our common suffering into hope for the future."

~ Nelson Mandela

"No act of kindness, no matter how small, is ever wasted."

~ Aesop

"The simplest acts of kindness are by far more powerful then a thousand heads bowing in prayer."

~ Mahatma Gandhi

"If you want others to be happy, practice compassion. If you want to be happy, practice compassion."

~ 14th Dalai Lama

"I've learned that people will forget what you said, people will forget what you did, but people will never forget how you made them feel."

~ Maya Angelou

There's a wonderful TED talk given by Benjamin Dunlap revolving around an incredible human being named

Sandor Teszler. Teszler reminded Dunlap of Mahatma Gandhi in orthopedics minus the loincloth, and briefly describes Teszler's upbringing and ascension. He describes how Teszler was ostracized as a child and endured multiple surgeries for his clubbed feet. He was then relocated to a German school for being a Jew, however, went on to build a successful textile firm with his brother in Yugoslavia, where none had previously existed.

One night, Teszler was summoned by a watchman, who'd caught an employee stealing socks. Teszler confronted the thief and asked, "But why do you steal from me? If you need money, you have only to ask." The night watchman, insisting they call the police, was stunned when Teszler said, "No, that will not be necessary, he will not steal from us again." Even as the Nazi campaign began infiltrating his hometown, and perhaps being too trustworthy, Teslzer remained in Yugoslavia.

As tensions rose, he prepared cyanide capsules for himself and his family to take in the event of capture. With the final solution in full swing, he and his family were arrested and relocated to a death camp on the Danube. During a particularly heinous beating, one of Teszler's children asked, "Is it time to take the capsules now, papa?" Hearing this, the man delivering the beating leaned down to Mr. Teszler and said, "No, do not take the capsules, help is on the way." In a twist of fate almost unimaginable, the man delivering the beating was the very thief on which Teszler had bestowed his compassion.

Compassion is one of the most beautiful human qualities, and it is no wonder that we show great admiration for those who express it well. They are the individuals that stand in the face of injustice, power, and fear. They are the men and women who give voice to the downtrodden and ease the burden of the less fortunate. They are the people that sacrifice for the betterment of the whole. Not only do they recognize the suffering of their fellow brothers and sisters, but they take action to alleviate that very suffering.

The reality of suffering is all around us. On the world stage, there are war, disease, famine, and natural disaster. In the more civilized locations, it fills our hospitals, jails, unemployment lines, and psychiatric wards. In everyday life, people struggle to pay the bills or maintain a grip on an adequate level of happiness. As stated in chapter two, nature would seem to have no compulsion to care for our ultimate success as a species, or in our attaining fulfillment.

On the whole, I think that most people are mostly good most of the time, otherwise how would we have made it as far as we have? But in the vast majority of instances, we can do a better job at making the world a more just and fulfilling place to live. Most of us have an intuition that the cure for most of the ills in the world is a large dose of empathy. It is thought that if we feel the suffering of others, we will in turn act. If we could place ourselves in the shoes of the victim, it would help cure all that ails us. But empathy, as we will see, has its limitations.

Many people confuse the terms "empathy" and "compassion," but they are really quite distinct. Empathy is simply the attempt to understand and experience the feelings of another, whereas compassion is the awareness of another's suffering and wanting to do something about it. Empathy can further be divided into subcategories of emotional and cognitive, where emotional empathy equates to feeling another's pain, and cognitive empathy is an understanding of it. Cognitive empathy is ethically neutral, as you can use your understanding of another's feelings in order to help or manipulate them. Emotional empathy, on the other hand, is typically seen as an unquestioned good and our lack thereof as a foundation for immorality and injustice. But there are limits and drawbacks to the practice of emotional empathy that prevent the most effective forms of reducing the sum suffering in the world.

In *Against Empathy*, psychologist Paul Bloom argues that because emotional empathy is narrowly focused, biased, and myopic, it tends to lead to negative outcomes. It is narrowly focused because it typically concentrates on individuals rather than groups, and it is made worse by the fact that there are limits to what we can effectively imagine. Biased because we typically only think of those in our immediate groups. And myopic as it tends to focus on the here and now rather than long-term effects. It has a tendency to ignore statistical data and can even spark violence when we empathize with one group over another. Empathy, of course, is not all bad and can serve a great purpose, but as with any emotion, it needs guidance.

Take charities as an example. Organizations around the globe receive donations largely as a result of people's empathy for the plight of others facing some specific issue or disaster. Many donations come in the form of clothing and food, which often goes to waste, never reaching those in need. What is more, time, energy, and money are wasted in dealing with the logistical issues of collecting, storing, and disposing of these unnecessary items. Even worse, empathy tends to make people think charities should operate on razor-thin budgets, thereby limiting salaries for those operating the charities. By devaluing the monetization of compensation and effectiveness, it dissuades the most talented individuals from seeking employment in these types of operations.

Some organizations like the Red Cross even take advantage of our empathy by asking to donate to a specific cause like the earthquake in Haiti or the tsunami in Japan with no intention of using those donations for that specific cause. Others go much further and operate purely as frauds. An outfit called Cancer Fund for America only spent around 3 percent (some accounts say less) of the 187 million dollars they received in direct aid, the remainder going to fundraising, purchasing cars, vacations, paying family salaries, etc. The emotionality of an issue can blind us to the reality, and it seems fairly obvious to me that what is missing from all this is a strong dose of rationality.

By no means should you stop giving to charitable organizations. They have been integral to the precipitous drop in many of the world's biggest issues such as infant mortality, poverty levels, and disease rates over the last fifty years. Beyond that, the amounts we give to charity as a nation and as individuals are absurdly low. But a higher level of scrutiny and research is needed prior to doing so.

Cost-benefit analysis and statistical data are rarely an impetus for people to become more charitable, but they are by far and away the best tools to illuminate the reality of an issue and correct it. Of course, it's easy to get lost in statistical data with correlation and causation issues or people attempting to skew the numbers. But we live in a world of data numbers and algorithms, and we should do our best to utilize them in order to illuminate the truth. For the truth, as we've all heard, shall set you free.

When empathy calls us to action, our emotionality can prohibit us from making the best use of our efforts. This is why using compassion, which is more diffuse and detached, is often a more effective tool in alleviating the suffering of the world. It lessens our emotional engagement, which causes us to make biased and short-term decisions. It engages our more rational qualities and helps us make more reasonable and effective decisions.

I certainly hope this doesn't sound uncannily detached from the reality of suffering in our world, as I truly do want to help make it a better place. There are certain dangers inherent in pure rationality, but it is our compassion, rather than our empathy, that helps us achieve the proper balance between emotionality and rationality when taking ethical actions. As philosopher David Hume said, "Reason is and ought only to be, the slave of the passions." But which passion we engage with and how we engage with it is critical to the desired outcome.

We must ask ourselves, how do we increase our compassion for and engagement with our fellow brothers and sisters? And I would argue, not just our fellow humans, but other conscious creatures as well. And why should we be concerned in the first place? First of all, we know for a certainty that helping other people is one of the easiest ways to increase your level of happiness.

Not only that, but giving, just like anything else, is subject to the law of reciprocity. The more you give, the more you receive. As for increasing your compassion, it partly comes from curiosity and knowledge. By educating yourself about the world or community you live in, you come into contact with unjust and unsustainable activities that attract your attention, thereby generating interest and action.

Another wonderful tool is through the practice of loving kindness meditation. Not only has it been shown to increase your compassion and contentment, but it also makes physical and functional changes to your brain, reducing stress and pain perception, increasing cortical folding, improving memory, decreasing negative emotional reactions, etc.

Furthermore, you need not make any metaphysical assumptions to begin the practice of meditation. It can act purely as an empirical exercise. If you do x, you will experience y. Though specific types of meditation can produce certain desired effects, they serve a limited function, as Sam Harris suggests in *Waking Up*. I'll therefore introduce you to a broader and more utilitarian type of meditation in the final chapter of this book.

For many, their legacy is their children; for others, it is their fortune or empire. But I would venture to argue that by far and away, the more powerful legacy is seen through the acts that we do for others and the difference we make in their lives. We truly build a legacy through our compassion for others. As William James said, "The deepest principle in human nature is the craving to be appreciated," and, "act as if what you do makes a difference, [for] the great use of life is to spend it for something that will outlast it."

CHOOSE GROWTH

VIII

"It is under the greatest adversity that there exists the greatest potential for doing good, both for oneself and others."

~ 14th Dalai Lama

"Do you think you should enter the garden of bliss without such trials as came to those who passed before you."

~ Quran

"If the people knew how hard I had to work to gain my mastery, it wouldn't seem wonderful at all."

~ Michelangelo

"Human progress is neither automatic nor inevitable... Every step toward the goal of justice requires sacrifice, suffering, and struggle; the tireless exertions and passionate concern of dedicated individuals."

~ Martin Luther King Jr.

"I am not discouraged because every wrong attempt discarded is another step forward."

~ Thomas Edison

~

Most have heard the expression "no pain, no gain" or Nietzsche's corresponding iteration "what doesn't kill you makes you stronger." But it seems to be a virtue generally lacking in our modern world of convenience and instant gratification. Success is difficult, and don't let anyone tell you otherwise. Bill Gates didn't take a day off from twenty to thirty. Warren Buffett started reading financial books when he was seven. Stephen King writes four hours every day. I want you to dispel any notion that getting what you want out of life comes easy. Additionally, you must recognize that life rarely responds to want or need, rather it responds to deserve. In the book *Outliers*, Malcolm Gladwell shows that the work is a given and that most successful people have about 10000 hours of experience. He also suggests that luck is a critical factor; be it timing, location, or connections, there are certain intangibles that are invariably part of the equation. But this is the lesson of the second commandment: do what you can, accept what you can't.

Of course, the principle of growth, like all others, admits of exceptions. Take the aforementioned luck. Some people, no matter how healthy their lifestyles will develop heart disease or cancer at an early age as a result of their genetic code. Air travel is amongst the safest forms of transportation on the planet, yet some number of people will be killed every year. Such are the laws of statistical probability. Furthermore, the expressions, "no pain no gain" and "what doesn't kill you makes you stronger" can't literally be true all the time. There are some experiences that can make you weaker, both physically and psychologically. But what we're interested in is post-traumatic growth and all the effective ways to guide and strengthen our character.

The analogy of physical strength fits perfectly here. In order for us to build muscle, we must apply tension, thereby breaking the muscle fibers down; the muscle may then reconstruct itself to be stronger and more resilient. We must give it the right nutrition and the proper rest. We can be students in order to become more effective or efficient. We can fail to learn the right methods and tools and be wasting our time. We can overexert and injure ourselves. These are analogous to the necessities required for personal growth, the cultivation of an environment conducive to achieving optimal results, and educating yourself in order to become more efficient and prevent failures.

The principle of action over theory is also apropos here, as no amount of blathering about health and fitness will actually make you stronger. Unapplied knowledge is worthless. This exercise metaphor also works well for teaching the practice of patience and the question of suitability. We can't expect to develop the physique of a model or the fitness of an Olympian overnight. Nor is every person cut out for such lofty attainments. If you're 4'10", I'm sorry, but you will not be playing in the NBA or NFL. You might just make it as a jockey, however.

Another apt metaphor, and one that I commonly use for myself, is that of a climber on a mountain. We all have goals, some loftier than others, but you must realize you have to climb the mountain. Some routes are harder than others, some impossible. Some mountains are only climbable by certain individuals. Some peaks seem unattainable, but when whittled down into manageable sections, it just becomes a process. "Step by step we get ahead," as Charlie Munger said. Sometimes you fall, sometimes you fail, but we use those experiences as a means of learning and growth. As the idiom goes, "Our greatest glory consists not in never falling, but in rising every time we fall."

Failure should be expounded upon here, as it's a huge factor. If we can reappraise failure as a learning experience and a means of growth, we can change our attitude and outlook. As Henry Ford said, "The only real mistake is the one from which we learn nothing." Or from Winston Churchill, "Success is stumbling from failure to failure with no loss of enthusiasm." We can use the tool of perspective as Mark Twain did when he said, "What is joy without sorrow? What is success without failure? What is health without illness? You have to experience each if you are to appreciate the other. There will always be suffering, but it is how you perceive your suffering and how you deal with it, that will define you."

We must address the issue of entitlement here, as it seems to be a growing concern. If you live in a modern society, almost every service and product you can imagine and consume is created for us at a low cost, absurd quantity, and ridiculous level of availability. Most of us have no inkling of the amount of resources, effort, and innovation it takes to produce the things we utilize in our consumer culture, and it is this very disconnectedness that helps perpetuate a sense of entitlement and a lack of personal responsibility. The food we eat, the clothes we wear, the electronics we use, and the litany of other products at our disposal should make your head spin. But of course, all these items are subject to the adaptation principle. Look around you and try to imagine having to produce all the things you utilize and take for granted. Imagine sourcing all the things that sustain your existence. You'll quickly find an easy and readily available source of humility and gratitude.

What are some of the most effective tools to help you grow? A great one is finding mentors. Seek, find, and contact people that have achieved what you want to accomplish. Spend time with them, learn from their mistakes, adopt their habits, and you'll drastically shorten your path to success. Don't listen to people that haven't accomplished what you're trying to do. Understand that action is the only thing that will ultimately allow you to succeed. As stated before, no amount of unapplied knowledge is useful. Learn the power of saying no. Say no to all the things that are slowing or preventing the achievement of your goals. Learn to create habits rather than relying on will power. Will power, like a muscle; will tire, but when a habit is created, the behavior becomes automatic. Realize the power of your surroundings. If you hang out with five rich people, you'll be the sixth. And of course, the corollary also applies as well, if you hang out with five poor people, you will be the sixth. Be willing to take risks. As Henry Miller says, "All growth is a leap in the dark, a spontaneous unpremeditated act without benefit of experience." Realize that motivation is garbage. Successful people do things whether they feel like it or not and feel amazing after.

There are some extremely lucky individuals out there that absolutely love what they do and say they never had to work a day in their lives. But they are the exception. Achievement is difficult, and it takes time, effort and knowledge.

If it wasn't clear in the opening paragraph, I want to ensure that the necessity of work in achievement can't be understated. Edison puts it wonderfully when he says, "Opportunity is missed by most people because it is dressed up in overalls and looks like work." Or take another of his pertinent maxims, "What it boils down to is one percent inspiration and ninety-nine percent perspiration."

Success in every arena, and in the vast majority of cases, is earned. It is earned by those who are willing to get out of their comfort zone and take a risk; it is earned by those individuals who use their own and others' failures as lessons; it is earned by those who are lifelong learners who realize that if you're not getting ahead, you're falling further behind. If you want wealth, power, respect, wisdom, or to achieve any other lofty goal, you must put your nose to the grindstone and get to work.

It couldn't be stated more clearly than when the famous violinist Itzhak Perlman was asked, "You know Mr. Perlman, I would give my whole life to be able to play the violin like you did tonight". He smiled and said simply, "I have".

BALANCE

IX

"It is better to rise from life as from a banquet - neither thirsty nor drunken."

~ ***Aristotle***

"Almost every wise saying has an opposite one, no less wise to balance it."

~ ***George Santayana***

"The best and safest thing is to keep a balance in your life, acknowledge the great powers around us and in us. If you can do that, and live that way, you are really a wise man."

~ ***Euripides***

"Happiness is not a matter of intensity but of balance, order, rhythm and harmony."

~ ***Thomas Merton***

"Evermore in the world is this marvelous balance of beauty and disgust, magnificence and rats."

~ ***Ralph Waldo Emerson***

The Chinese philosophy of the Yin and Yang symbolizes how seemingly opposing forces are complementary and interconnected. How does one appreciate the light without experiencing the dark? How can there be good without evil, order without chaos, or life without death?

The commandments themselves are an attempt at finding the balance of certain opposing forces. They are about striving for harmony both internally and externally. They strive to uphold the best aspects of selfishness and selflessness. The practice of growth, which requires pressure, must be balanced with love and compassion. The practice of gratitude must be balanced with the perspective of reality. Living in the now must be balanced with preparing for the future. Our affinity for caring for family must be balanced with the care for strangers. We must balance our emotionality with reason, work with play, exertion with rest, and so much more.

Of course, not all the factors listed here are necessarily opposing. Often, we need to balance one attribute amongst multiple recipients. We should express love, gratitude, and compassion to everyone, but to say that a stranger should receive the same amount as your child is certainly overstating the case. In a strictly Darwinian calculation, and as JBS Haldane famously joked in response to a question about whether he'd give his life to save a drowning brother, he said, "No, but I would to save two brothers or eight cousins." Furthermore, opposing forces won't necessarily require equal distribution. Should we strive to spend half our time working on ourselves and half the time for others? Should we allocate half our time for work and half for leisure? To some extent, these questions will be answered for us by the nature of each of our current realities. There are millions of people not fortunate enough to even comprehend leisure time, let alone attempt to achieve some sort of balance between it and work. In other instances, these questions of quantity will have to be answered by the individual or society.

Some forms of balance we can safely say need adjustment in one direction or another. For instance, our cognitive biases and emotionality can be great barriers to our being objective when thinking about any given proposition; it is therefore safe to say that we should do more as individuals and as a society to use the tools we know to be effective at combating our irrationality. In the balance between emotionality and rationality, we need to skew towards a more rational existence.

What is more, there are some instances where it should be perfectly acceptable to say that striving for zero tolerance is the most balanced approach, such as the proliferation of nuclear weapons or keeping narcotics out of the hands of children. Like there is a continuum of responsibility in specific behavioral traits between nature or nurture, there is a continuum of balance between which value should be applied and in what amount. For the most part, our instincts do well in guiding us here, for as I said before, I think that most people are mostly good most of the time. But we must continue to illuminate all those "lowly stamps of our origin" and commit to combating our natural ineptitudes and irrationality, while conversely developing methods of sustaining and improving our noblest attributes.

In order to elucidate the necessity of balance, I've intentionally placed contradicting advice in this book. You are to accept certain things and change others, to express compassion but apply pressure, to remember how bad it could be and yet be grateful for just how good it is. When the need to think critically arises, Carl Sagan said it best, "It seems to me what is called for is an exquisite balance between two conflicting needs: the most skeptical scrutiny of all hypotheses that are served up to us and at the same time a great openness to new ideas. Obviously, those two modes of thought are in some tension. But if you are able to exercise only one of these modes, whichever one it is, you're in deep trouble."

Even the indisputable truth of the next chapter calls for a certain kind of balance. It is always now, and we should do everything we can to enjoy the present moment, but that doesn't mean we should stop preparing for the future or reflecting on the past. Having and accomplishing certain goals is one external pleasure that we know can make you lastingly happier. Reflecting on and learning from our past is also necessary. These goals often preclude us from taking the most enjoyable route in the present. We all understand that discovering the happy medium between reflecting on the past and having a desirable destination is notoriously difficult, but again, it's finding the balance that matters.

There is also the ever-raging battle of progress versus custom, which takes place in political parties, social movements, organizations, etc. It is not that either side is correct, but where the balance lies and on which issue, as each should be considered individually. Socialism vs. capitalism, freedom vs. equality, competition vs. cooperation, concentration of wealth vs. redistribution of opportunity – these debates have been taking place for thousands of years, as Will Durant suggests in *The Lessons Of History,* and again, it's finding the balance rather than choosing sides of either opposing force that is crucial to our success.

As we can see, finding the balance of distribution in a certain ethic or the balance of opposing forces is paramount to successfully navigating the path to building a just and thriving individual or society. We need not be discouraged by the difficulty of the task at hand or cry apathy for the glacial pace of our progress, for history suggests that our advancement, though not continuous, is palpable and real. We must not lose sight of the forest for all the trees and understand that the vast majority of the answers we seek and even our happiness, as author and social psychologist Jonathan Haidt suggests, lies in between.

KNOW IT'S ALWAYS NOW

X

"Happiness, not in another place but this place...not for another hour, but this hour."

~ ***Walt Whitman***

"Realize deeply that the present moment is all you ever have."

~ ***Eckhart Tolle***

"Wherever you are, be there. If you can be fully present now, you'll know what it means to live."

~ ***Steve Goodier***

"If you are depressed, you are living in the past. If you are anxious you are living in the future. If you are at peace, you are living in the present."

~ ***Lao Tzu***

"The past is already gone, the future is not yet here. There's only one moment for you to live."

~ ***Buddha***

~

As the saying goes, there's no time like the present, but that needs to be changed. As a matter of experience, there is no time BUT the present. It shouldn't be *carpe diem* (seize the day) as Horace suggested; it should be *carpe nunc* (seize the now). It is always now, and now is your only opportunity to: be happy, take that dream vacation, write a book, lose weight, ride an alpaca, design a sustainable and organic line of garden gnome ornaments or anything else you've ever wanted to accomplish in life). This moment truly is your only opportunity. *Fac si facis*, do it, if you're going to do it.

Sam Harris puts it exquisitely in a speech entitled *Death and the Present Moment* where he said,

> *The reality of your life is always now and I think this is a liberating truth about the nature of the human mind, in fact I think there is probably nothing more important to understand about your mind than that if you want to be happy in this world. The past is a memory. It's a thought arising in the present. The future is merely anticipated. It is another thought arising now. What we truly have is this moment, and this. And we spend most of our lives forgetting this truth, repudiating it, fleeing it, over looking it. And the horror is that we succeed. We manage to never really connect with the present moment and find fulfillment there because we are continually hoping to become happy in the future, and the future never arrives.*
>
> *~Sam Harris*

Living this lesson, not just knowing it, is one of the most powerful truths one can realize in life. Hence why it is the final chapter of this book.

We should expand on the subject of death, and speak to its obvious importance. Harris continues in his speech that most people tend not to think about death, while religions like to pretend that it is not real. The first group does their best to keep the reality of death out of view by assuming that if you just keep your foot on the gas until you run out of road, everything will be fine. Religions, on the other hand, tell us that the most important events we'll experience occur after our death.

Both these modes of thought are grounds for ignoring the reality of the situation we find ourselves in, and I find this type of thinking dangerous and dogmatic. If we are to assume that the power to change our reality lies outside our control, and that this life is merely a placeholder for a reality beyond the material world, then our civilization is surely destined for failure. Alternatively, if you assume that death is real, and there are many well-established truths that lead us to this conclusion, you will find yourself attempting to make the best use of the only life that you can be sure of. Death and taxes are certain but so is taking advantage of the present moment to do something more.

I can't tell you what happens after death, and anyone that tells you that they can is either selling you something or lying to you. But in all probability, it is just like before you were born: nothingness. Everything we know about the brain suggests that it is at the very least involved and highly suggestive that it creates the entirety of our conscious awareness. And although we don't understand exactly how consciousness arises from neurochemical events in the brain, we can safely assume that it is just like any other process in the universe.

Take fire for instance. Fire requires four things, three of which we're all familiar; combustible material, oxygen, and heat. The fourth and final element is a sustained chemical reaction. If you remove one of these ingredients, the fire doesn't go anywhere, the process just stops. In all probability, consciousness, like fire, is just another process. Furthermore, the brain's functionality, on many levels, is divided into parts, and if we destroy one part, we lose some particular functionality. Why would you assume without evidence that if you destroy the whole thing, as happens upon death, all that functionality escapes the bonds of the material world and transports itself completely undetected or undisturbed to some place beyond space and time? It's simply unwarranted.

Science is not closed to the idea of consciousness surviving the death of the brain; there are just no good reasons at present to justify that conclusion. The beauty of scientific thinking is that it allows us to incorporate new information and improve its understanding of how the universe actually works. Religion is on the losing side of an ever-raging battle with the facts of our existence and is actively preventing our progress as a species by continuing to support and propagate untenable dogmas. Though many people consider changing your stance on any given matter a character flaw, science's ability to adapt is a feature, not a bug. Just think for instance where we'd be if we still believed that the world was flat, or didn't understand the germ theory of disease.

The lesson of our ultimate death and the understanding that it is always now helps us to realize that time is our most valuable resource. If you live to the ripe old age of seventy-five, you'll have approximately 27,394 days with which to accomplish all that you desire. Of course, we need to subtract several years in youth, a few golden years, and the time you spend sleeping.

Let's be generous and say you start chasing your dreams at eighteen, you only have ten years on easy street during your twilight, and that you sleep eight hours a day. Now you're left with a paltry 11,444 days. I also imagine the vast majority of my audience is over eighteen, so if we assume you're the average age of an American, which is thirty-eight, that leaves you with, and I'm sorry to say, a minuscule 6,574 days to experience all that this wondrous life has to offer. That is only eighteen years of useful time in one's life...the end is nigh at hand indeed.

We must understand that we are never getting more time and we must do all in our power not to waste it. We must endeavor to use it wisely, living these and other important lessons. We must encourage others to do the same. We must concern ourselves with discovering and upholding the most honorable uses of our time. And recognize, as the Tibetan saying suggests, that, "If you take care of the minutes, the years will take care of themselves."

If you've not realized it already, let me remind you that everything is temporary. Over 99 percent of all species on this planet no longer exist, and the sun will eventually expand as it runs out of hydrogen, destroying Earth in the process. Even every mental state you've found yourself in and every thought you've ever had – it's all temporary. This can be disconcerting, and the cynic believing all is for naught would have us become a nihilist. But when you understand that this life is all you can count on, you have a very compelling reason to make the most of it. Choosing to see these facts in another light makes us embrace the beauty, profundity, and fleeting nature of life. As the Buddha says, "Ardently do today what must be done. Who knows? Tomorrow, death comes."

Other sage advice in this arena was touted by Shakespeare when he said, "Things won are done, joy's soul lies in the doing." And from Albert Einstein, when he said, "I never think of the future, it comes soon enough." They are trying to teach us that it is always now and you should only focus on the journey, not be looking towards a destination.

How do we incorporate these lessons, and what tools can we use to engage with them more frequently? Oftentimes, our lack of courage, confidence, or conviction makes us hesitate. Our fear of failure or looking foolish inhibits us from taking action. We find fruitless our ability to motivate ourselves and procrastinate in accomplishing our desires. But if you incorporate the Latin motto "fortune favors the bold" or you "just do it" as Nike suggests, you can then correct course along the way and later be asking yourself, why didn't I do this sooner?

We tend to mistakenly think that success occurs in a straight line, but it is destined to meander along the way. Again, you will make mistakes, but by using mentors to avoid the large setbacks and relabeling failure as learning, you're well on your way to achieving your goals.

The TED talk "*How to stop screwing yourself over*" given by Mel Robbins is a must watch. In it, she suggests that you must stop hemming and hawing and clearly define what you want; that getting what you want is simple but not easy; that, within reason, you should never sell yourself short and think that you can't attain your goals; that motivation is garbage, and you'll never truly feel like doing what you need to in order to accomplish what you want. You must, therefore, force yourself to take action and overcome that initial tendency to choose comfort rather than growth.

To my knowledge, the most effective tool for teaching the lesson of the present moment is meditation. And as fortune would have it, it helps us to practice all of the lessons in this book. It can help you become the best version of yourself. It can help you gain the wisdom to accept what you can't change and take action on what you can. It can help you be more loving, practice positive reciprocity, find perspective, choose gratitude, cultivate compassion, grow, and discover balance. Pretty powerful, I'd say.

Meditation has been around for a long time, but its appearance and practice in the western world is relatively recent. One of its best features is that it can be taught in an entirely secular way; you need not make any assumptions about deities or metaphysical claims in order to practice. It operates on a purely empirical basis: if you do x, you will experience y.

Bringing a mindfulness practice into your life can pay huge dividends. It can lower stress, increase contentment, reduce negative emotional reactions, decrease pain perception, lower blood pressure, and so much more. One wonders why everyone isn't doing it. One of the best methods to utilize when beginning a meditation practice would be with Vipassana, which means "insight into the true nature of reality." Like most things worth doing, meditation is simple to describe yet difficult to accomplish. You concentrate on your breath, or other bodily sensations, and pay attention to the flow of experience. Thoughts will appear and be recognized in consciousness and then disappear or be replaced by other thoughts. But you simply return to the breath, other bodily sensations, and the flow of experience. By recognizing that thoughts are transitory appearances in consciousness, you come to understand that you are not the thinker of your thoughts, but the consciousness that is aware of them. You can thereby be free of them in principle. Simple, right?

It's this very inability to recognize thoughts as thoughts that produces the lion's share of the suffering we experience in our mental lives. Bad memories, insults hurled our direction, or fretting over something not said or done are all thoughts that arise in your conscious awareness. But thoughts are, by their very nature, fleeting and evanescent, and disappear as soon as you let them. Mental states are, of course, affected by physical ones, such as when you're tired, hungry, or injured, but how we frame those sensations can have a large impact on how we cope with them. If you can reappraise the situation for what it is – a temporary sensation appearing in consciousness – and you are actively doing all in your power to alleviate the sensation, you can relax and discover a place of peace.

Mindfulness meditation is one of the most powerful tools that we can incorporate into our daily regimen. It can help us let go of recurring negative thoughts and emotions, relieve our anxiety, and diminish our neuroticism. What is more, it allows us to find a place of peace and fulfillment within ourselves. Even if these moments of bliss are short-lived, their value is incalculable. Over time, they can be increased in number and duration, thereby raising our aggregate state of contentment. If we can train our minds to identify with our awareness rather than our thoughts, we can then be free to enjoy whatever is occurring in the present moment, which, to repeat myself, is all you'll ever have.

EPILOGUE

As stated in the opening paragraph of this book, our survival is obviously our prime directive, and it governs much of our behavior. But as a species, we have a distinct opportunity to engage with and pursue a goal beyond that of mere survival. That goal is also quite obvious, and it is the goal of attaining fulfillment.

Why do we do the things we do, consume the things we consume, and say the things we say? Every action we take is an attempt to alter our conscious perception and create or repair a world we want to live in, and all around us, we find the evidence of our success and failure. As Plato pointed out many among us are sleep walking through life, and worse they know it and continue to do so.

Again, we mustn't assume that the task of raising our personal and social standards is too difficult, or resign ourselves to the fact that we will never achieve perfection. Though progress is slow and hard-won, at times stagnant or even regressive, we must bear the burden as individuals, as a society, and as a species to encourage the growth of the sum fulfillment of all sentient beings.

We must begin with ourselves before we may help others. We must shift our perception from victim to leader. We must surround ourselves with people that hold us accountable. We must realize that it is our duty, not a deity's, to make this world a better place. And we need a framework to govern our behavior that avails itself to all that we know.

As a global civilization, that framework is ever more becoming science, but as our scientific knowledge is incomplete and not fully disseminated, nor fully trusted by all, we also need the guidance of history, custom, culture, and law. We need a framework that avails itself to the lessons of our ancestors and the wisdom they left behind.

The preceding ten commandments form just that: a framework combining the wisdom of the ages with the knowledge of our modern world. A framework within which we can attempt to build an inclusive and just form of human solidarity – a solidarity that maximizes fulfillment and minimizes suffering, a solidarity that allows humanity to flourish and reach its true potential.

Of course, there is a multitude of other ethical principles that are not contained within the bounds of this book, and by no means does that make them irrelevant to the conversation. Things like honor, consent, and sacrifice all belong in a framework humans follow in order to thrive as individuals and as a society. They are critical elements in maximizing human fulfillment. But this book was written for the generalist, and I could only touch on certain aspects important to living a good life (and I am sure I missed some altogether). Some of that was intentional and some of it was not; after all, I don't have all the answers. But I do have some really good ones.

I'm a huge fan of taking enormous and complex concepts such as ethics and boiling them down to their essence. As stated in the introduction, life is complex, but your philosophy towards it needn't be. What is more, as long as you're not cheapening the wisdom, it's best to get to the point. Every so often in one's life, we should take a step back and look at the bigger picture. Every so often, if we want to appreciate the forest, we need to step back and stop contemplating all the trees.

I firmly believe that the scientific process will eventually answer most of the questions we have about the fundamental properties of the known universe, including how to live a long, unique, and incredible human life. I also understand that there are important questions that may never be answered, and new questions will constantly appear that challenge our current concept of reality. For some that's disconcerting, but for me, it's part of the beauty of being alive. The unknown elicits a sense of wonder and curiosity, and brings forth an undiscovered country to be explored, understood, and appreciated.

I told you in the beginning that this was a story of forgiveness, hope, and redemption. It is a story of forgiving ourselves the mistakes of the past and the "lowly stamp of our origins." It is a story of hope for taking humanity's most timeless wisdom and availing ourselves to all that science has discovered. It is a story of redemption for me, but only time and our actions will tell if it is ultimately a story of redemption for us all.

This story and all the others we tell ourselves bring meaning and value into our lives. Through understanding and implementing all of the available wisdom of the past and present, we can build lives truly worth living. By cultivating our best traits and strengthening the bonds we form with others, we can truly know what it means to be fulfilled.

There are so many incredible and awe-inspiring things in this world, and helping others to discover and value them is an integral part of my life's purpose. I want you to know how amazing it feels when you truly appreciate your existence. I want you to experience the sheer brilliance of life. I want you to feel the joy of being.

I sincerely hope that the knowledge contained within this book has stirred a deep-seated desire within you – an impulse to go venture out into the world and make it a better place in whatever way you can. I hope its wisdom is useful in helping you discover and share your gifts. I hope it has enriched your life and can function as a tool in helping you become the best version of yourself. I hope, As Ralph Waldo Emerson said, "... to know even one life has breathed easier because you have lived." That is my hope. That is my redemption.

If I have succeeded, I shall be filled with nothing but gratitude and continue to believe that we can ALL rise to the occasion and save ourselves from ourselves!

SO ... WHAT NOW? ... WHAT COMES NEXT?

Are you ready to take the next step? Are you ready to begin your journey towards becoming the best version of yourself ? Are you willing to put in the the time and effort necessary to build the life you've always wanted?

Are you ready to start living life with, and on purpose?

If so ...

Please visit http://www.ABetterTen.com/ and sign up for our email list. We will constantly be adding new content and begin offering free giveaways and practical tips on how to incorporate these commandments into your life. We will also offer additional information and products and how to live a more fulfilled life, so please stay tuned for all that is to come.

If you care to know more about the author visit:

http://ABetterTen.com/about-the-author/

If you would like to inquire about media contacts

http://ABettertTen.com/contact/

If you enjoyed the book, and would care to share your thoughts please leave a review on Amazon.

Last, and certainly not least, if you know someone that would benefit from this book, please share it with them. Give them the gift and the opportunity to live life with, and on purpose.

Love and Respect

James Miller

BIBLIOGRAPHY

- Aurelius, Marcus, *Meditations,* Naxos AudioBooks, Unabridged edition, May 4, 2010
- Bloom, Paul, *Against Empathy: The Case for Rational Compassion*, Harper Audio, Dec. 6, 2016
- Bloom, Paul, *Just Babies: The Origins of Good and Evil*, Random House Audio, Nov 12, 2013
- Bryson, Bill, *A Short History of Nearly Everything*, Books on Tape, Oct. 17, 2003
- Buss, David, *Evolutionary Psychology: The New Science of the Mind*, Psychology Press; 5th edition, Nov 20, 2014
- Campbell, Joseph with Moyers, Bill, *The Power of Myth*, Anchor, June 1, 1991
- Coyne, Jerry A., *Why Evolution is True*, Audible Studios, Sept 2, 2009
- Dawkins, Richard, *The God Delusion*, Mariner Books; Reprint Edition, Jan 16, 2008
- Gladwell, Malcolm, *Outliers: The Story of Success*, Little, Brown & Company; Unabridged Edition, Nov 18, 2008
- Haidt, Jonathan, *The Happiness Hypothesis: Finding Modern Truth in Ancient Wisdom*, Gildan Media, LLC Jan 3, 2007

- Harris, Sam, *The End of Faith*, Simon & Schuster Audio, Mar 13, 2008
- Harris, Sam, *Letter to a Christian Nation*, Simon & Schuster Audio, Nov 17, 2006
- Harris, Sam, *The Moral Landscape: How Science Can Determine Moral Values*, Simon & Schuster Audio, Oct 5, 2010
- Harris, Sam, *A Guide to Spirituality Without Religion*, Simon & Schuster Audio, Sept 9, 2014
- Hitchens, Christopher, *God is not Great: How Religion Poisons Everything*, Hachette Audio, April 27, 2007
- Keller, Gary and Papasan, Jay, *The One Thing: The Surprising Simple Truth Behind Extraordinary results*, Rellek Publishing Partners, Ltd., Oct 8, 2013
- Lieberman, Daniel E., *The Story of the Human Body: Evolution, Health, and Disease*, Random House Audio, Oct 1, 2013
- Voogd, Peter, *6 Months to 6 Figures*, Game Changers Inc., Mar 24, 2015

REFERENCES

Tim Spector. Identically Different: Why We Can Change Our Genes, The Overlook Press, Peter Mayer Publishers, Inc. 2013

Israel Finklestein and Neil Asher Silberman, The Bible Unearthed: Archaeology's New Vision of Ancient Israel and the Origin of Its Sacred Texts, Free Press, 2001

Andrew E. Hill, John H. Walton, A survey of the Old Testament 2000

Shermer, Michael "Why are we moral: The evolutionary origins of morality" The Science of Good and Evil. New York: Times Books 2004

Peter Singer, Ethics and Intuitions, The Journal of Ethics 2005

Haidt, Jonathan. "The emotional dog and its rational tail: A socialintuitionist approach to moral judgment." Psychological Review, 108, 814-834. 2001

Wikipedia contributors. "List of cognitive biases." Wikipedia, The Free Encyclopedia. Wikipedia, The Free Encyclopedia, 28 Jul. 2017. Web. 31 Jul. 2017

Wilkinson, G. (1984). "Reciprocal Food Sharing in the Vampire

Bat" Nature. 308 (5955): 181–184. Bibcode:1984 Natur. 308..181W.-doi:10.1038/308181a0.

Flower, T, Gribble, M, Ridley, A. Deception by Flexible Alarm Mimicry In An African Bird, Science, 02 May 2014: Vol. 344, Issue 6183, pp. 513-516

Bartal, I. B.-A., Decety, J. & Mason, P. Empathy and Prosocial Behavior in Rats, Science 334, 1427–1430 (2011).

Wechkin, S., Masserman, J.H., and Terris, W. Jr.: "ALTRUISTIC" BEHAVIOR IN RHESUS MONKEYS. The American Journal of Psychiatry Vol 121. Dec. 1964. 584-585.

de Waal, F. B. M. & Davis, J. M. Capuchin cognitive ecology: cooperationbased on projected returns, Neuropsychologia, 1492, 1–8, 2002

Gesquiere, Laurence R.; Learn, Niki H.; Simao, Carolina M.; Onyango, Patrick O.; Alberts, Susan C.; Altmann, Jeanne "Life at the Top: Rank andStress in Wild Male Baboons". Science. 333 (6040): 357–60, 2011

Christopher, R, Cacilda, J, Sex At Dawn: The Prehistoric Origins ofModern Sexuality, Harper; 1 edition, June 29, 2010

Begon, M.; Harper, J. L.; Townsend, C. R. Ecology: Individuals, populationsand communities Blackwell Science, 1996

Clutton-Brock, T. H., Parker G. A., Punishment in animal societies,Nature 373, 209 - 216, 19 January 1995

Kohn, Alfie No Contest: The Case Against Competition. Houghton Mifflin Harcourt. 1992

Okasha, S. (2008). "Biological altruism". The Stanford Encyclopediaof Philosophy. Retrieved July 20, 2013.

de Wall, F.B.M., Do Animals Feel Empathy, Scientific American Mind, 2007

Hrdy, D. B. "Infanticide as a primate reproductive strategy". American Scientist. 65 (1): 40–49, 1977

de Wall, F.B.M., Good Natured: The Origins of Right and Wrong inHumans and other Animals, Harvard Univ. Press, Cambridge, Massachusetts, 1996

Bloom, P. Against Empathy: The Case for Rational Compassion. Ecco, 2016

Robinson, M, Are People Naturally Inclined to Cooperate or Be Selfish? Scientific American Mind, 2014

Rozin P, Haidt J, & McCauley C.R., Disgust In M. Lewis & J.M. Haviland-Jones (Eds) Handbook of Emotions, 2nd Edition (pp637- 653). New York: Guilford Press, 2000

De Almeida, Rosa Maria Martins; Cabral, João Carlos Centurion; Narvaes, Rodrigo, "Behavioural, hormonal and neurobiological mechanisms of aggressive behaviour in human and nonhuman primates". Physiology& Behavior. 143: 121–35, 2015

Tajfel, H. "Experiments in intergroup discrimination (abstract)". Scientific American. Springer Nature. 223: 96–102, 1970

Brickman P, Coates D, Janoff-Bulman R., Lottery winners and accident victims: is happiness relative, Journal or Personality and Social Psychology: 8-917-27 1978 Aug

WHO, UNICEF, World Bank Group, UN-DESA Population Division, joint news release, UN: Global child deaths down by almost halfsince 1990, 13 September 2013

W.A. Spooner, "The Golden Rule," in James Hastings, ed. Encyclopedia of Religion and Ethics, Vol. 6 (New York: Charles Scribner's Sons, 1914) pp. 310–12, quoted in Rushworth M. Kidder, How Good People Make Tough Choices: Resolving the Dilemmas of Ethical Living, Harper,New York, 2003. p. 159. Simon Blackburn also notes the connectionbetween Confucius and the Golden Rule. Simon, Blackburn 2001

Ethics: A Very Short Introduction. Oxford: Oxford University Press. p. 101.

Kvanvig, Helge Primeval History: Babylonian, Biblical, and Enochic: An Intertextual Reading, BRILL, 2011

Lichtheim, Miriam Ancient Egyptian Literature, Volume II: The New Kingdom. University of California Press. p. 147, 2006

Gerald S. Wilkinson, Reciprocal food sharing in the vampire bat, Nature 308, 181 - 184, 08 March 1984

List-Dugatkin, L. A. Cooperation Among Animals: An Evolutionary Perspective, Oxford Univ. Press, 1997

Olendorf, Robert, Thomas Getty, and Kim Scribner. Cooperative Nest Defence in Red–winged Blackbirds: Reciprocal Altruism, Kinship or By–product Mutualism? Royal Society Publishing, 22 Jan. 2004. Web. 14 Sept. 2014

Tomasello, M., The ultra-social animal, Eur. J. Soc. Psychol., 44: 187–194., 2014

Kaplan, Hill, Lancaster, Hurtado, A Theory of Human Life History Evolution: Diet, Intelligence, and Longevity, Evolutionary Anthropology, 2000

Female Genital Mutilation/Cutting: A Global Concern, New York: United Nations Children's Fund, February 2016.

CIA, The World Factbook, https://www.cia.gov/library/publications/the-worldfactbook/geos/af.html, July 31, 2017

Sankaran, L, Caste Is Not Past, The New York Times Sunday Review, Jun. 15, 2013.

PEW Research Center, World Population by Income: How Many Live on How Much, and Where, July 18, 2015. http://www.pewglobal.org/interactives/global-population-by-income/, July 31, 2017.

De Neve, Jan-Emmanuel and Christakis, Nicholas A. and Fowler, James H. and Frey, Bruno S., Genes, Economics, and Happiness, CESifo, Working Paper Series No. 2946, August 2012

Emmons RA, et al. "Counting Blessings Versus Burdens: An Experimental Investigation of Gratitude and Subjective Well-Being in Daily Life, "Journal of Personality and Social Psychology: Vol. 84, No. 2, pp. 377–89, Feb. 2003

Seligman MEP, et al. "Empirical Validation of Interventions," American Psychologist: Vol. 60, No. 1, pp. 410–21. July–Aug. 2005

Rick Hanson PhD, Confronting the Negativity Bias, Psychology Today, Oct 2010

Baummeister, Bratslavsky, Finkenauer, and Vohs, Bad Is Stronger Than Good, Review of General Psychology Vol. 5. No. 4. 323-37, 2001

Eric Mosley and Derek Irvine, The Power of Thanks,Mcgraw-Hill, 2014

Justice, B&J, Grateful-ology: Science and research on gratitude, Health Leader, https://www.uthealthleader.org/story/grateful-ology, July 31, 2017

Seppälä, E, 18 Science-Based Reasons to Try Loving-Kindness Meditation, Oct. 1, 2014, https://www.mindful.org/18-science-based-reasonsto-try-loving-kindness-meditation/, Jul 31, 2017

Positive Psychology Program, The 23 Amazing Health Benefits of Mindfulness for Body and Brain, Mar 6, 2017, https://positivepsychologyprogram.com/benefits-of-mindfulness/, Jul. 31, 2017